From Rome to the World

The Epic Leadership of Pope Leo I

by

Dr. ant

From Rome to the World: The Epic Leadership of Pope Leo I

Contents

Introduction

In the annals of history, there emerges a figure of such towering influence that his legacy transcends the corridors of time. Such a paragon is Pope Leo the Great. Born in an era shrouded in tumult and transformation, Pope Leo did not merely participate in the epochal events of his day; he emerged as a defining force, a bulwark of Christian orthodoxy, and a shepherd to a flock beset by both external perils and internal discord.

Yet, to comprehend the full scope of Leo's significance, one must first understand the wider backdrop of the declining Roman Empire. With the imperial edifice in disarray and the once-mighty Roman legions failing to repel barbarian invasions, chaos seemed inevitable. However, amidst this crumbling facade stood Leo, not merely a bishop of Rome, but a potentate of unparalleled spiritual and temporal authority.

In his tenure as the Supreme Pontiff, he championed the doctrinal purity of the Church with untamed zeal. When heresies such as Eutychianism threatened to distort the faith's tenets, Leo's voice was a clarion call, defending orthodoxy with eloquent theological rebuttals. His tome to the Council of Chalcedon remains a testament to his unwavering commitment to doctrinal clarity, a masterpiece of theological precision that earned him the appellation of "Doctor of the Church." His words, etched in the annals of ecclesiastical councils, resonate with an authority that even emperors could not ignore.

But Leo was not confined to the realm of theologian alone. His prowess as a diplomat was nowhere more evident than in his famed encounter with Attila the Hun. Through an unparalleled combination of spiritual gravitas and political acumen, Leo managed to dissuade the Scourge of God from sacking Rome, thus preserving the heart of Christendom from certain ruin. One cannot overstate the dramatism and tension of such moments. These were not simply historical anecdotes; they were defining episodes that shaped the fate of Western civilization.

For a man vested with such immense responsibility, Leo's vision was strikingly clear. His ecclesiastical reforms sought to fortify the Church's structure, ensuring that both clergy and laity adhered to principles that enhanced the community's moral and spiritual fabric. His reign saw efforts to discipline wayward priests and laity, balancing justice with pastoral concern, seeking a Church reflective of its divine calling.

Moreover, Leo's impact was not restricted to the realm of theology and politics; his influence permeated the social and cultural milieu of his time. As an advocate for Christian art and literature, he championed the expression of faith through beauty, inspiring a legacy of devotion that would be immortalized in frescoes, manuscripts, and architectural marvels. His eloquent sermons, replete with rhetorical finesse, illuminated the hearts and minds of his contemporaries, guiding a society amidst the throes of metamorphosis.

In examining Leo's theological contributions, one discerns a titan who stood firmly in the Augustinian tradition, while also innovating and expanding the doctrinal horizons of the Church. His writings reflect a synthesis of philosophical musings and practical wisdom, underscoring the indivisibility of divine truth and human reason. These texts, suffused with a depth that belies their temporal inception, continue to inspire theologians and laypersons alike.

Leo's rapport with the Eastern Churches further illustrates his significance in fostering ecclesiastical unity amidst prevailing doctrinal disputes. His diplomatic correspondence with patriarchs and emperors exemplifies a leader not of mere local importance, but of ecumenical stature. Leo's efforts in bridging the divides that threatened Christian unity underscore a statesman whose influence extended beyond the Roman See, impacting the universal Church.

In terms of liturgical reforms, Leo's contributions were both profound and enduring. He sought to imbue the Church's rites with a sacrality that reflected divine majesty and historical continuity. His introduction of new rites and liturgical innovations sought to preserve the sanctity of worship, ensuring that the celebration of the divine mysteries remained an encounter with the transcendent.

Furthermore, Leo's dedication to education and the preservation of knowledge signified a commitment to intellectual rigor and spiritual depth. His initiatives in enhancing clerical education underscored a belief in the transformative power of knowledge. By preserving ancient texts, Leo ensured that the wisdom of the past would illuminate the path of the present and future generations.

The challenges faced by Leo were manifold. Internally, the Church grappled with doctrinal schisms and political intrigues. Externally, the deteriorating socio-political landscape of the Roman Empire posed existential threats. Yet, amidst these trials, Leo's fortitude and spiritual leadership remained unwavering, a testament to his divine calling.

Indeed, the legacy of Leo the Great cannot be encapsulated within the confines of a single narrative. His canonization as a saint and his recognition as a Doctor of the Church bespeak a life lived in profound communion with the divine. The process of his canonization, a testament to his sanctity, underscores the enduring veneration in which he is held by the faithful.

As we embark upon a deeper exploration of Pope Leo the Great, let us endeavor to appreciate the myriad dimensions of his legacy. More than a historical figure, Leo the Great stands as a beacon of faith, wisdom, and courage. His life and works continue to inspire, challenging us to reflect upon the eternal truths that undergird our faith and our understanding of the world.

Chapter 1: The Early Life of Pope Leo I

The dawn of Saint Leo's life was imbued with divine foresight, marking the advent of a figure destined for greatness within the annals of Christendom. Born into the twilight of a crumbling Roman Empire, young Leo's heart was swiftly enkindled by a fervor for the faith, kindled not by fleeting fancy but by a profound and consuming zeal. As the tapestry of his early years unravels, one discerns the threads of a sacred calling—woven from the pious influences of devout mentors and the inexorable guidance of Providence. Such august beginnings did not merely shape his character; they forged an indomitable spirit, poised to navigate the trials and tempests that lay ahead. It is here, in the crucible of his nascent days, that the foundation was laid for a life of unparalleled theological rigor and unswerving commitment to the Church's universal mission.

Early Influences on Pope Leo's Faith

In the warm cradle of Tuscia in central Italy, young Leo, later hailed as
Pope Leo the Great, began his voyage of faith and fortitude. From the
nascent days of his existence, a divine tapestry seemed woven around him,
a blend of fervent belief and profound providence. The early prayers
echoed by his devout parents filled the air, imparting whispers of
reverence and sanctity. Imagine, if you will, a home filled with piety,
where the day's labors ended in solemn supplications and earnest readings
of Holy Scripture.

From his father, Quintianus, Leo inherited a robust sense of duty and
unwavering commitment to the precepts of the Christian faith. Quintianus
was a paragon of virtue, esteemed among his peers for his devoutness and
moral rectitude. He instilled in young Leo the cardinal virtues of
prudence, justice, temperance, and fortitude, which would later become
the cornerstone of his papal reign. In conversations, over meals, and
through example, Quintianus emphasized the importance of living a life
congruent with the teachings of Christ. It was within these formative
conduits that Leo's spirit was forged with steely resolve and profound
devotion.

Not far from their abode, the burgeoning Christian communities, still
fresh from the edicts of Constantine, served as fertile ground for the
young Leo's spiritual curiosity. These communities, burgeoning and
brimming with the vigor of unshackled faith, played an instrumental role
in his formative years. The hymns sung, the communal prayers, and the
liturgical practices etched indelible markings upon his soul. These early
ecclesiastical experiences provided a foundation upon which his
theological acumen and pastoral sensitivities would flourish.

Additionally, Leo's mother, often deemed the silent disciple in scriptural
exegesis, contributed significantly to his early spiritual tutelage. Her piety
was palpable, her prayers fervent, and her teachings gentle yet resolute.
She embodied the essence of the Beatitudes, instructing her son in the
ways of mercy, meekness, and purity of heart. Her stories of saints and

martyrs animated the walls of their home, turning it into a sanctum of veneration and holy inquiry. Thus, entwined in his mother's gentle hymns and his father's disciplined religious observance, Leo's faith was weaved with threads of fortitude and humility.

A noteworthy influence upon young Leo, extending beyond the immediate periphery of his household, was the local clergy. The priests and bishops he encountered were exemplars of devotion and erudition. They became both mentors and conduits through which divine mysteries were unraveled. The eloquence of their homilies, the solemnity of their ceremonies, and their unwavering dedication to pastoral care served as a beacon, guiding Leo toward his spiritual destiny. Their vibrant discussions on doctrinal matters ignited his intellectual curiosity, nudging him towards deeper theological inquiry and reflection.

The intellectual climate of the late Roman Empire also bore upon Leo's nascent faith. Classical education was not bereft of divine implications but rather interwoven with it. In his scholarly pursuits, Leo found himself drawn to the works of early Church Fathers and classical philosophers. The rhetoric of Cicero, the ethical precepts of Seneca, and the theological treatises of Origen further molded his spiritual and intellectual framework. The syncretic blend of classical wisdom and Christian doctrine fortified his understanding and articulation of faith.

Yet, it was not merely through intellectual and familial mediums that influences permeated Leo's young soul. The palpable presence of God in nature also played a vital role. The serene landscapes of Tuscany, with its undulating hills and verdant meadows, served as a continuous reminder of the Creator's magnificence. In these tranquil escapes, Leo often found a sanctuary for meditation and prayer. The rustling leaves whispered divine secrets, and the radiant sunsets painted visions of celestial glory, reinforcing his burgeoning faith.

As Leo came of age, his ecclesiastical journey intertwined with the broad tapestry of ecclesial polity and doctrinal evolution. He stood at the crossroads of a transformative age, where the remnants of paganism were gradually eclipsed by the luminous light of Christianity. The Church, overcoming its infancy marked by persecution and martyrdom, was solidifying its orthodoxy through councils and creeds. Leo absorbed these monumental shifts with ardent attentiveness, shaping his conviction and later, his papal agenda.

The notable influence of early Christian writers cannot be understated. Writings of Tertullian, Cyprian, and Augustine rendered a theological and spiritual compass for Leo. Their writings did not merely serve as doctrinal guides but animated his reflections and homilies. The theological profundity of Augustine's Confessions, the pastoral clarity of Cyprian's letters, and the apologetic fervor of Tertullian fortified his faith, turning theoretical knowledge into actionable belief.

In the crucible of these multifaceted influences, Leo's early religious framework was not left untouched by the trials of adversity. The social and political disturbances of the late Roman Empire, with barbarian incursions and internal strife, demanded a response from local ecclesiastical leaders. It instilled in Leo a practical theology that balanced contemplative faith with active service. He learned that faith was not merely an inward conviction but a call to outward action and societal engagement, a divine commissioning to lead by example.

Through the confluence of familial piety, ecclesiastical mentorship, intellectual rigor, and the natural splendor of his surroundings, Leo's faith blossomed into an enduring testament of divine providence. These formative experiences collectively forged a spiritual leader who would, in time, become one of the most influential pontiffs in the annals of the Church. Therefore, it is through understanding these early influences on Leo's faith that we truly grasp the genesis of his eventual greatness.

The seamless interplay of tender familial guidance, rigorous intellectual pursuit, and immersive ecclesial experience crafted the foundation upon which the edifice of his papal accomplishments was built. Leo's faith, while profoundly personal, was etched and shaped by the communal and historical realities of his era, preparing him to uphold and defend the faith with an indomitable spirit. Through the amalgamation of these influences, he emerged as a beacon of unwavering faith, unswerving in his commitment to the Church's mission and resolute in the face of heresies and political turmoil.

Education and Formation of Pope Leo's Character

Pope Leo I, also known as Leo the Great, emerged from an epoch brimming with doctrinal conflicts, social upheavals, and the ebbing strength of the Roman Empire. Such a time necessitated a mind both sharp and replete with virtue, one capable of navigating the turbulent confluence of spiritual and temporal realms. It was within this crucible that Leo's character was forged, a character deserving of the papal throne and the challenges that lay thereon.

In his early years, Leo benefitted from an education steeped in both classical and religious instruction. This duality of learning imbued him with a profound understanding of sacred texts alongside the rhetorical and philosophical teachings of the likes of Cicero and Aristotle. When studying the Holy Scriptures, his instructors emphasized not merely the letter but the spirit of the text, encouraging him to fathom the divine mysteries therein. This melding of secular and sacred knowledge endowed Leo with a potent intellectual arsenal, one that he would wield with great effect throughout his pontificate.

Moreover, Leo's mentors intently fostered a spirit of humility and service in him, virtues that were paramount in his personal development. The young Leo learned the importance of forgoing personal ambition for the betterment of the Church and its followers. Through acts of charity and devotion, he began to manifest a piety and commitment that would later underpin his papal decrees and sermons.

This education was not confined solely to the realm of the mind but extended into the practicalities of ecclesiastical administration. During his formative years, Leo acquainted himself with the workings of the Church's hierarchy and governance. Serving as a deacon in Rome, he was privy to the intricacies of Church operations, financial stewardship, and pastoral care. These experiences were pivotal, preparing him for his eventual role as the Supreme Pontiff. The responsibilities bestowed upon him during these years allowed him to translate theoretical knowledge into effective practice.

Leo's early mentors—those stalwart guardians of faith—played a decisive role in crafting his character. Among them were scholars and clerics whose wisdom spanned generations. They imparted not only theological rigor but also an unwavering conviction in the Church's role as the custodian of divine truth. This mentorship was instrumental in shaping Leo's later theological pronouncements, especially in his defense against heresies and the development of Church doctrine.

In addition, the socio-political tumult of his youth further cemented his resolute spirit. Witnessing the decline of the Roman Empire and the chaos that ensued, Leo became acutely aware of the Church's pivotal role as a stabilizing force. These experiences fortified his resolve to strengthen and purify the Church. His later life bore testament to the lessons he garnered during these years, as he ceaselessly worked to bolster the Church's spiritual and moral authority amid external threats.

Yet, it was not solely his education that shaped Pope Leo's character; his personal disposition and innate virtues also played a crucial role. From a young age, Leo exhibited an innate sense of justice and an unyielding commitment to truth, qualities that distinguished him among his peers. He was known for his eloquence, a gift that would later serve him well in his sermons and writings. This rhetorical prowess was not merely an attribute but a tool he wielded to convey complex theological ideas with clarity and conviction.

In his relationship with God, Leo experienced a depth of communion that transcended mere intellectual assent. His prayer life was marked by fervor and intimacy, undergirded by a profound trust in Divine Providence. This spiritual depth was the foundation upon which all his actions as Pope were built. He understood that leadership in the Church was not just about governance but about being a shepherd to the faithful, guiding them towards the eternal truth.

As his academic and spiritual formation progressed, Leo began to internalize the dual imperative of orthodoxy and orthopraxy—right belief and right practice. This synthesis became evident in his later theological works where he seamlessly integrated doctrine with pastoral care. His ability to articulate complex theological principles in a manner that was accessible to the lay faithful underscored his commitment to nurturing the Church's spiritual life.

Indeed, the formation of Pope Leo's character was an amalgamation of divine providence, rigorous education, and lived experience. His mentors and the ecclesiastical environment provided fertile ground for the development of his theological acumen and pastoral sensitivity. Through his diligent study and service, Leo cultivated the virtues of wisdom, humility, and fortitude, all of which would be indispensable in his later role as Pope.

Additionally, Leo's exposure to the crises of his time—both internal ecclesiastical conflicts and external pressures—sharpened his decision-making abilities. He learned to navigate these crises with a balance of firmness and compassion, ensuring the unity and sanctity of the Church. This pragmatism, combined with his theological insight, made him an effective and revered leader.

The spiritual and educational formation of Pope Leo stands as a testament to the holistic approach needed for ecclesiastical leadership. His life serves as a paradigm for the integration of intellectual, pastoral, and spiritual disciplines, demonstrating that true leadership in the Church arises from a profound union with God and a deep understanding of the human condition.

Thus, while the annals of history are replete with the achievements of Pope Leo the Great, it is in his early education and character formation that we discern the roots of his greatness. His life invites contemporary leaders to emulate his example of disciplined learning, humble service, and unwavering faithfulness to the Church. Leo's formative years, therefore, are not merely a prelude but a blueprint for enduring ecclesiastical leadership.

In summation, the education and formation of Pope Leo's character were the crucible in which his abilities and virtues were refined. These formative years laid the foundation upon which he would build his legacy, a legacy that continues to inspire and guide the Church to this day.

Chapter 2: The Rise of Pope Leo I

As the smoke of the ancient city swirled with the murmurs of divine providence, there emerged from the august halls of the Holy See a figure destined to etch his name indelibly upon the sacred annals of history. Leo, who was not born to the purple of imperial lineage, yet bore the unmistakable mantle of chosen servitude, ascended to ecclesiastical eminence through a divine orchestration that bewildered the mortal imagination. His initial role within the Holy Church marked by a dutiful commitment saw him navigating the tapestries of doctrinal discourse and pastoral care with unyielding resolve. But it was in the year of our Lord 440, when the celestial decree proclaimed him Supreme Pontiff, that Leo the Great commenced his meteoric rise. With a resolve as firm as the ancient Roman columns, he unified the faithful, fortified the dogmas of the Church, and grappled with heresies that gnawed at the very fabric of Christianity. In this crucible of divine and terrestrial struggle, Leo emerged not merely as a shepherd to his flock, but as a towering bulwark of theological and moral conviction, whose influence would ripple through the corridors of Christendom for centuries hence.

Pope Leo's Initial Role in the Church

As we turn to the chronicles of the early life of Leo, who would ascend to the papal throne and take the venerable name Pope Leo I, one cannot overlook the humble yet pivotal inception of his ecclesiastical journey. Long before he grasped the reins of the papacy, Leo's influence began to permeate the ecclesiastical fabric of the Roman Church. He was a deacon of Rome, a position accompanied by considerable responsibility and honor, denoting a man whose capabilities had been recognized far and wide.

It was during these early days that Leo first began to exhibit the traits that would later mark his papacy: a profound grasp of theological matters, an unwavering dedication to the Christian doctrine, and an extraordinary eloquence in his homilies. These were not attributes cultivated in isolation but were fostered within a community brimming with faith, scholarship, and devotion. This community proved fertile ground for a man of Leo's discernment and ambition.

Unlike the unobserved stars scattered across the deep night sky, young Leo's talents did not go unnoticed. The ecclesiastical authorities of Rome were quick to realize that Leo was no mere custodian of holy orders but a beacon of doctrinal purity and moral rectitude. Consequently, he was appointed to positions that required both intellect and administrative acumen. As deacon, he managed the Church's temporal affairs, an assignment that gave him firsthand experience in the complex interplay between spiritual leadership and temporal governance. This duality of roles was not only a testament to his versatility but also a crucible in which his leadership qualities were tempered and proven.

Throughout this period, Leo worked closely with several illustrious churchmen, including the then Supreme Pontiff, Pope Sixtus III. His proximity to generations of papal wisdom provided him a unique perch from which to observe and learn the nuances of church leadership. The lessons gleaned from these liaisons were invaluable, adding layers of depth to his understanding of both the sacred and the profane.

The ecclesiastical environment of Rome during Leo's early years was fraught with doctrinal disputes and myriad challenges that threatened to disrupt the unity of the Church. Gnostic and Pelagian heresies were rampant, and the Church needed champions who could articulate orthodox beliefs with clarity and authority. Leo was often called upon to engage in theological debates to defend the orthodoxy. His defenses against heretical teachings were marked by astuteness, a clear articulation of Christian doctrine, and an unyielding stance on matters of faith.

Leo's diplomatic skills, honed in the nursery of ecclesiastical responsibility, were showcased when he served as an emissary of the Church to the imperial court. He was a sage interlocutor, skilled in the art of negotiation and diplomacy. His eloquence and persuasiveness not only facilitated successful missions but also curried favor and goodwill from secular powers, a fundamentally critical asset for the Church's survival and expansion in tumultuous times.

Among his early notable achievements was his role in the dispute between the Church of Rome and the Patriarch of Alexandria. Here, Leo demonstrated a remarkable ability to mediate, arbitrate, and, when necessary, assert the primacy of the Roman See. His interventions played a crucial role in preserving the doctrinal integrity and hierarchical unity of the Church, setting the stage for his later confrontations with more formidable ecclesiastical adversaries.

In those early formative years, Leo's spirituality and intellectual prowess attracted the attention of many, including laypeople and clergy alike. He forged alliances and cultivated friendships that would later prove beneficial during his papacy. His networks extended far beyond Rome, reaching into the furthest corners of Christendom. These relationships were not just instrumental but indicative of Leo's approach to leadership —a blend of wisdom, humility, and strategic acumen.

Pope Leo's initial role can thus be seen as a confluence of preparation and providence. The early assignments that he undertook were all, in a sense, preparatory steps to a grander stage. They were a crucible, refining his abilities and fortifying his resolve for the challenges that lay ahead. In retrospect, Leo's roles before his papacy were not just important responsibilities; they were stepping stones laid by divine guidance leading to his ultimate vocation.

Through a tapestry woven with threads of theological rigor, administrative acumen, and unyielding faith, young Leo adorned his nascent ecclesiastical career. Each responsibility he assumed, each theological debate he engaged in, each negotiation he carried out, progressively etched the contours of a leader who would eventually be revered as Pope Leo the Great. In the dim-lit corridors of Rome's basilicas and the bustling forums of the imperial court, Leo honed the skills that would make him not only a pivotal religious figure but also a venerated saint whose impact reverberates through the annals of Church history.

Thus, as we delve deeper into the chronicles of Pope Leo I, it becomes increasingly evident that his initial role in the Church was no mere prelude but the very foundation upon which his legacy as Pope Leo the Great was built. Each act, each decision in those formative years, was imbued with the latent potential that would blossom into monumental significance. Leo's early ecclesiastical journey stands as a testament to the divine orchestration of destiny, heralding the rise of one of the most influential popes in Christendom.

Pope Leo Becomes Supreme Pontiff

The journey of Leo to the pinnacle of ecclesiastical authority commenced with an acclamation that echoed through the sacred halls of Christendom. His ascent to the esteemed office of Supreme Pontiff was marked not by mere circumstance but by the indelible conviction that he was divinely chosen in a tumultuous epoch. The ecclesiastical landscape of his time was fraught with doctrinal disputes and schisms, compelling Rome to seek a leader of unwavering faith and judicious temper.

Upon the death of Pope Sixtus III, the papal throne was not merely vacant but was seen as a beacon requiring a resolute guardian. Leo's reputation as a defender of the faith and a prudent diplomat had long been established through his previous offices, rendering him a suitable candidate in the eyes of both the clergy and the laity. As the Church deliberated, Leo, then archdeacon, resided on a mission in Gaul mediating a formidable dispute that bore both political and spiritual ramifications.

The canonical election transpired swiftly. Ecclesiastical envoys conveyed the unanimous decision, urging Leo to return posthaste to Rome. His arrival was met with immense fervor and solemn ceremonies. Yet, the weight of his new mantle was not lost on him. From the moment the papal tiara was placed upon his head, he epitomized the shepherd ready to combat wolves threatening his flock.

Leo's enthronement was more than a mere liturgical act; it was the embodiment of the Church's hope amidst an era riddled with uncertainties. His investiture was celebrated with grandeur and reverence, reflecting the profound significance of his new role. These ceremonies were imbued with tradition, symbolizing continuity and divine ordination. With his investiture, he became the vicar of Christ on Earth, the mediator between the divine and the mortal.

The new pontiff was cognizant of the formidable responsibilities that lay ahead. His oratorical prowess and theological acumen were well-regarded, yet he understood that the papacy was as much an earthly office as a spiritual one. To govern a Church—and by extension, an empire—in turmoil required sagacity surpassing the mere guidance of doctrine.

Leo's immediate concern was to restore unity within the Church and assert the doctrine against manifold heresies. His approach was both pastoral and authoritative, wielding the power of persuasion and the decree with equal measure. His era demanded a delicate balance of firmness and diplomacy, and Leo embodied this with unerring precision.

The writs, decrees, and letters of this early period of his pontificate reveal a man deeply committed to the theological purity of the Church. He issued proclamations that reinforced the Nicene Creed, directly addressing the Arian and Pelagian controversies that had sown discord. By aligning with the true teachings of the Church Fathers, Leo fortified the dogmatic foundations that would influence Christendom for centuries.

In his pastoral care, Leo was unwavering. He took keen interest in the moral and spiritual welfare of his congregants, ensuring that the sacraments were administered with utmost sanctity. The pontiff's sermons resounded with the fervor and clarity that left no room for ambiguity. His homilies, steeped in exegesis, were instrumental in guiding the faithful and rebutting theological errors.

On the administrative front, Leo embarked on reformist measures that injected rigor into the clerical order. The hierarchy of the Church was rejuvenated with principles of discipline and moral rectitude. Bishops and clergy were reminded of their vows and responsibilities, emphasizing the need for personal sanctity and public virtue. This ecclesiastical reformation was as much about restoring confidence in the Church as it was about doctrinal integrity.

Pope Leo's tenure was opportune, coinciding with immense geopolitical upheaval. As the Western Roman Empire teetered on the brink of collapse, rapid changes in political landscapes necessitated a Pontiff capable of both spiritual and temporal governance. Leo's diplomatic acumen was soon put to the test, but that is a tale for another chapter. His legacy within the hallowed walls of the Vatican began with firm grounding and unwavering resolve.

Leo's ability to harmonize spiritual doctrine with practical governance provided the firm bedrock upon which his papacy would sculpt monumental theological and ecclesiastical advancements. The fervent allegiance from his bishops and the deep veneration from his laity bore testament to his divine ordination as the Supreme Pontiff.

Thus, Pope Leo I's ascension was not just a historical inevitability but a divine providence. His pontificate, inaugurated with solemnity and grandeur, stood as a bastion of faith, unity, and doctrinal purity. Henceforth, the chronicles of his papacy would underscore his immense contributions and the steadfast spirit with which he steered the ship of the Church.

Chapter 3: Pope Leo IÃ¢Â□Â□s Theological Contributions

In the annals of ecclesiastical erudition, Pope Leo the Great emerges as a luminary of theological profundity. His contributions to the sacred tomes of doctrine were numerous and immeasurably significant, fortifying the sanctified teachings of the Church against the insidious wiles of heresies. With unparalleled zeal, Leo ofttimes asserted the dual nature of Christ, both divine and human, a doctrine which he solidified through eloquent epistles and fervent homilies. His epistle to Flavian, known as the *Tome of Leo,* became a cornerstone at the Council of Chalcedon, anathematizing heretical views and reaffirming orthodox belief. Moreover, his theological insights extended beyond mere defense; he ventured into the realms of elucidation and amplification, thereby crystallizing Church teachings that would resonate through the centuries. In such pursuits, Leo's intellect and divine inspiration reigned supreme, bequeathing to the Church a legacy that would steadfastly guide the faithful through tumultuous epochs.

Defense Against Heresies

The annals of history acclaim Pope Leo I not merely as a pontiff but as a bulwark against the insidious tides of heresy that threatened the sanctity of the nascent Church. In an epoch fraught with doctrinal tumult and theological discord, his heroic defense emerged as a fortress of orthodoxy, standing steadfast against the ceaseless onslaught of heterodox teachings.

Under the shadow of Rome's declining imperial glory, the Christian Diocese braced itself against myriad doctrinal aberrations. Pope Leo's acumen in theological clarity shone brightly in this celestial contest, dispelling the darkness of confusion that sought to envelope the faithful. One cannot overstate the gravity of his interventions, as they cemented the essence of Christian dogma for generations yet unborn.

A most notable heresy of the time, the Nestorian controversy, plunged the Church into a maelstrom of debate over the nature of Christ. Nestorius, Patriarch of Constantinople, promulgated a distinction so severe between Christ's human and divine natures that it risked bifurcating the singular essence of the Savior. Pope Leo's Tome—a missive to the Council of Chalcedon—eloquently articulated the doctrine of the hypostatic union, reaffirming the indivisible yet dual natures of Christ. Through his discerning words, unity was restored to the ecclesial community, extinguishing the fiery discord.

Equally pressing was the menace of Eutychianism, which swung the doctrinal pendulum to the opposite extreme. Eutyches posited that Christ's human nature was absorbed or subsumed by His divine essence, thereby compromising His true humanity. Upon receiving word of these pernicious teachings, Pope Leo swiftly penned letters and dispatched legates to the concerned councils, delineating the orthodox position—that of Christ being both fully divine and fully human, yet one Person.

Through his relentless efforts to address these theological perils, Leo the Great undertook a role akin to that of a vigilant shepherd, guarding his flock from doctrinal wolves. The Synod of Chalcedon, held in 451 A.D., stands as a monumental testament to his theological prowess. Here, his letters were read and acclaimed, giving birth to the Chalcedonian Definition, a creed that fortified the orthodoxy of Christological tenets.

But beyond the celebrated councils and formal debates, Leo exhibited a pastoral zeal that permeated his writings and sermons. His words served as an anodyne to the faithful while correcting those misled by false teachings. The eloquence of his homilies brought solace and certainty to a beleaguered congregation, reinforcing that the immutable truths of the faith were under divine guardianship.

Importing an unerring sense of duty, the pontiff extended his vigilance over matters of lesser-known but equally dangerous heterodoxies. The Priscillianist and Manichaean sects, though considered minor by some, warranted Leo's unswerving attention. Each was rebutted with theological precision, leading to their gradual extinction in the realms of Christendom.

Pope Leo did not merely confront these heresies with polemics or an array of epistles. He approached the task with a spiritual depth that underscored his entire pontificate. For him, the defense of doctrine was not merely a matter of intellectual rigor but one of profound spiritual warfare. His prayers and fasts were inseparable from his theological engagements, embodying his belief that the battle against heresy was indeed a battle for the souls of the faithful.

Moreover, Leo realized the importance of ecclesiastical unity in the face of such heretical threats. His correspondence with other bishops and leaders across Christendom engendered a unified front, strengthening the Church's ability to rebuff divergent doctrines. This unity not only solidified the theological stance of the Church but also acted as a bulwark against the fragmentation that heretical movements often precipitate.

His theological efforts also carried political ramifications. By defending orthodoxy, Pope Leo bolstered the Church's moral authority, which in turn allowed it to navigate the turbulent political waters of the time with greater efficacy. His actions demonstrated that theological clarity was intrinsically linked to the Church's ability to contend with external pressures and internal schisms alike.

The oeuvre of Pope Leo I provides a timeless guide for those grappling with doctrinal dissensions. His writings, an amalgamation of theological insight and pastoral concern, continue to instruct and inspire. They remind us that the path to orthodoxy, though fraught with conflict, remains indispensable for the health and unity of the Church.

In summation, the defense against heresies during Pope Leo's tenure is not merely a reflection of his intellectual and spiritual acumen but a testament to his indomitable spirit. Through his unwavering commitment to doctrinal purity, Leo the Great ensured that the essence of Christian faith was preserved with crystalline clarity, endowing subsequent generations with a legacy of unyielding orthodoxy.

Development of Church Doctrine Under Pope Leo

Behold, how in the hallowed times of Pope Leo the Great, the sacred fabric of Church doctrine found new adornment and sturdier threads. His time as Supreme Pontiff marked a renaissance in ecclesiastical thought, a profound exploration and consolidation of tenets that etched themselves indelibly upon the firmament of Christian orthodoxy. Through storms of theological discord and quagmires of heresies, Leo's sagacious navigation charted a resolute course.

As waves of doctrinal controversy crashed against the bulwarks of the Church, the edict of the Chalcedonian Council in AD 451 stood as a monumental testament to Leo's theological acumen. Cardinal to its decrees was the "Tome of Leo," a document crafted with such eloquent rigor and blessed precision. Composed by Leo himself, this tome became the lodestar that guided the Council to affirm the dual nature of Christ—both fully divine and fully human—a mystery woven into the very fabric of Incarnation.

The Bishop of Rome, with wisdom akin to that of Solomon, embraced a theological vision both ancient and progressive. Acknowledging Christ's dual nature wasn't a mere academic exercise; it was wrestling with the divine and human elements that thread through the Church's very essence. Leo's contributions thus solidified an understanding that would serve as the bedrock upon which future theological explorations could safely rest. His ability to distil complex theological debates into comprehensible and orthodox statements was unparalleled.

What makes Leo's contributions even more poignant and arresting is his uncanny ability to blend pastoral care with theological exactitude. Each letter, each sermon, carried the weight of theological innovation, yet never abandoned the heartfelt pastoral concerns of his flock. This combination rendered his doctrinal developments not distant, impenetrable treatises but living and breathing tenets accessible to every soul who sought divine truths under his stewardship.

It was during this period of dogmatic crystallization that Pope Leo, in sagacious repose, sought to combat the heresies that threatened to unravel the Christian fabric. Nestorianism and Eutychianism are but names gesturing at storms of theological confusion—heresies that Leo untangled with divine insight. His epistles and encyclicals became the sword and shield against these disruptions, affirming the immutable truths that stood resilient.

One particular corner of Leo's doctrinal tapestry was his profound emphasis on the centralized authority of the Papacy, which he viewed not merely as a position of power but as a sacred trust. Drawing from the Petrine doctrine, Pope Leo asserted the primacy of the Bishop of Rome as the cornerstone of ecclesiastical unity. This was no mere political stance but a theological conviction grounded in the belief that unity underpinned the Church's ability to withstand doctrinal fragmentation.

In Leo's world, the harmony of the Church wasn't an abstract ideal but a tangible, living reality—one that needed the guiding hand of a shepherd. His articulation of papal primacy was both authoritative and profoundly pastoral, reiterating that the seat of Peter held the keys not only to paradise but also to the coherence of Christian truth on earth.

As the array of his contributions further unfolded, it became evident that Leo's theological enterprises were not confined to Christological specifics and hierarchical structures alone. His engagement with the broader issues of sin, redemption, and grace also enriched the theological landscape. These doctrines, elaborated with finesse and echoed through his pastoral writings, underscored the inherent dignity of human nature in its redeemed state.

The drama of salvation, so passionately unfurled by Leo, presented the faithful with a vivid tapestry of divine mercy and human cooperation. In the crucible of his thought, Leo melded the sublime truths of human fallibility with divine omnipotence, painting a coherent picture of salvation that served to elevate the spiritual aspirations of his contemporaries and posterity alike.

Pope Leo's theological measures were not just reactions but full-fledged formulations that anticipated and prevented future schisms. His foresight, therefore, acts as a safeguard, not just an antidote. By strengthening ecclesiastical doctrines, he precluded the future ecclesial ruptures, ensuring that the unity he so dearly championed would endure through tempests and trials of subsequent ages.

Of particular note is Leo's contribution to Marian theology, which he approached with both humility and reverence. His reverence for Mary as Theotokos (Mother of God) in the face of heretical disputes wasn't merely scholastic; it emanated from a deep-seated faith that sought to honor the role of the Virgin Mother in the grand divine plan. Leo wasn't content with abstract titles; he invoked Mary with a pastoral affection that mirrored the devotion of the faithful.

Thus, by stitching the divine mysteries of Christology, soteriology, and Marian orthodoxy into a unified fabric, Leo showcased a masterful blend of intellectual robustness and spiritual fervor. His theological contributions extended a tapestry wide and far, a rich inheritance for both contemporaries and future Christians.

Pope Leo's legacy in the development of Church doctrine transcends the annals of history, finding resonance in the eternal truths that define Roman Catholic orthodoxy. His theological articulations served to fortify the Church against the heterodox winds that would seek to tear its doctrinal sails. Under his watchful eye, the barque of Peter sailed steadily, navigating through reefs of heresy and the stormy seas of doctrinal discord, arriving at a haven of divine truth and unity.

Chapter 4: Political Leadership and Diplomacy

Pope Leo the Great, with a visage both resolute and sagacious, stands unparalleled in the annals of diplomacy and political prudence. His tenure, marked by an era of seismic shifts and looming calamities, reveals the intricate tapestry of his leadership. Leo's deft maneuvering amidst the waning days of the Roman Empire showcased his uncanny ability to wield moral authority whilst navigating the tempestuous seas of statecraft. His encounter with Attila the Hun remains enshrined in the chronicles, a testament to his bravery and eloquence, which turned the tide of invasion through sheer force of conviction. In these dire epochs, Leo's actions were not merely the exertions of a pontiff; they were the orchestrations of a grand symphony composed to preserve both the temporal and spiritual realms. Thus, Leo emerges not solely as a spiritual shepherd but as a beacon of political acumen, a paragon whose legacy in diplomacy endures through the corridors of history.

Pope Leo's Role in the Decline of the Roman Empire

The decline of the Roman Empire was a tumultuous period marked by sociopolitical upheaval, economic strife, and external threats. Amid these chaotic times, the figure of Pope Leo I (Leo the Great) stands as a beacon of moral authority and shrewd diplomacy. His ecclesiastical reign intersected significantly with the political and social currents of his era, shaping not merely the Church but the broader Roman polity. In this complex tapestry, Pope Leo's contributions must be evaluated with the gravitas they deserve.

As Rome weakened, it demanded robust leadership. The Western Roman Empire, besieged by barbarians and internal decay, found in Leo both a spiritual guide and a temporal diplomat. Leo's leadership was not merely symbolic but actively engaged in the empire's intricate political affairs. He understood that the Church, while transcendent, must also operate within the realms of human governance and civic duty.

Pope Leo's capacity for diplomacy is epitomized in his encounter with Attila the Hun in 452 A.D. Rome was on the brink of devastation as Attila advanced, imbued with a ferocity that had already laid waste to great swaths of Europe. Leo, with quiet resolve and profound eloquence, confronted the Hunnic leader. The meeting's specifics remain shrouded in a blend of history and hagiography, but its outcome is indisputable: Attila retreated, sparing Rome a horrific fate.

In an era when military might often overshadowed spiritual counsel, Leo's success with Attila illustrated a profound shift. Leo demonstrated that moral suasion and steadfast faith could rival and even surpass armed force. This moment illuminated the power of the papacy as a stabilizing force during Rome's decline, underscoring the Church's role in temporal governance.

Leo's engagement in the empire's political machinery extended beyond isolated incidents. He navigated a labyrinth of factions, both secular and ecclesial, advocating for unity and doctrinal purity. His sermons and letters convey a dual audience—addressing both the spiritual needs of his flock and the administrative exigencies of the state. Through these communications, he reinforced the notion that the Church's health was intertwined with the empire's stability.

Another vital aspect of Leo's political acumen was his approach to the Roman aristocracy. During his pontificate, the elite still wielded substantial influence, both in Rome and throughout the provinces. Recognizing this, Leo engaged them not as adversaries but as potential allies. He fostered relationships that emphasized the mutual benefits of collaboration, aiming to fortify the Christian fabric of the empire against encroaching pagan influences and internal dissension.

Moreover, his theological assertiveness also impacted Rome's political landscape. Leo's adamant stance against heresies, such as Eutychianism, was not mere doctrinal rigidity but a strategic effort to consolidate ideological unity. He posited that orthodoxy was a bulwark against the morass of Rome's political fragility. In essence, heresy bred division, while orthodoxy fostered cohesion.

The Council of Chalcedon in 451, where Leo's Tome played a pivotal role, is another testament to his far-reaching influence. The council's decrees sought to unify a fractured Christendom, indirectly reinforcing the political unity of the empire. Leo's deft theological articulations provided clarity, aiding the imperial agenda of unity, even as Rome's political borders continued to contract.

However, the decline of the Roman Empire was complex, driven by myriad factors, many beyond the purview of any one individual. Economic distress, military losses, and administrative corruption all played their inexorable roles. Yet, Leo's contributions can be seen as the glue attempting to hold together the disintegrating pieces of the Roman mosaic. His temporal and spiritual leadership offered a semblance of stability, a moral compass for a society adrift.

In the sphere of law and order, Leo also made his mark. His advocacy for the Roman legal tradition, infused with Christian ethics, aimed at preserving the remnants of Roman jurisprudence. He saw the law not as a relic of a bygone era but as a living framework that could evolve to meet the needs of a Christianized Rome. Thus, through legal reforms and administrative oversight, he sought to buttress the empire's collapsing structures.

Leo's actions during the Vandal sack of Rome in 455 further underscore his role in tempering the decline. Although unable to prevent the sack, his negotiations with the Vandal leader Genseric resulted in a less catastrophic outcome than might have transpired. His intercession preserved churches and sacred sites, directing a modicum of respect toward Rome's Christian heritage even amidst the pillage.

In reflecting upon Pope Leo's role in the decline of the Roman Empire, one must appreciate the multiplicity of his efforts. He did not merely react to the exigencies of the moment but sought to shape the broader narrative of decline into one of resilience and adaptation. His endeavors provided a scaffold upon which the remnants of Rome could cling, paving the way for the eventual rise of a new, medieval Christian order.

Leo's legacy, thus, is woven into the fabric of Rome's decline. He represented a fusion of spiritual authority and astute diplomacy, wielding both the crosier and the olive branch with equal proficiency. By affirming the Church's role in the temporal realm, he heralded a new era in which the papacy would ascend as a pivotal force in European politics. Pope Leo's intricate dance amidst the crumbling vestiges of the Roman Empire remains a testament to his profound impact on history.

In summation, Pope Leo I's role in the decline of the Roman Empire exemplifies a paradox of strength and vulnerability. His leadership offered a path through the twilight of an era, illuminating how spiritual tenacity and political acumen can interlace to shepherd a society through its darkest hours. His legacy, revered and studied, continues to inspire as a paradigm of leadership amid adversity.

Negotiations with Attila the Hun

In the era marked by the shadows of a collapsing Roman Empire, loomed
the imposing figure of Attila the Hun, a scourge of God to some, and to
others, a test of divine providence. As the mantle of imperial power
waned, the Church, under the steadfast guidance of Pope Leo the Great,
emerged as a beacon of hope. Amidst the turbulence and tumults of these
times, one occasion stands out: the diplomatic encounter between Pope
Leo and Attila the Hun, a parley that would become legendary in the
annals of history.

The year was 452 AD, and the Huns, under the command of Attila, swept
across the European plains with an almost supernatural ferocity. Their
march, inexorable and unrelenting, brought desolation to many cities. As
their eyes turned to Rome, the eternal city trembled. Attila, with his
reputation as a ruthless conqueror, seemed an unstoppable force, a
tempest with intentions as dark as the storm clouds above. The imperial
power, fractured and feeble, could scarce hope to parry such a foe,
leaving a vacuum only spiritual gravity could fill.

Pope Leo, a man of profound intellect and unyielding faith, understood
the dire straits in which Rome found itself. The walls of the Church, built
upon the rock of Saint Peter, would now serve as the bulwark against this
impending calamity. In an act that combined divine inspiration with
masterful diplomacy, Leo decided to confront the barbarian king,
bringing to bear not just the weight of temporal authority, but the gravitas
of spiritual supremacy.

Accompanied by a contingent of Roman dignitaries, Pope Leo ventured to
meet Attila by the banks of the river Mincio, near Mantua. This encounter,
cloaked in an aura of suspense and solemnity, bespoke immense bravery.
The image of Leo, garbed in the vestments of his holy office, contrasting
with the fierce and worldly visage of Attila, struck a scene both dramatic
and significant.

History does not furnish us with a detailed account of their dialogue, but the outcome is renowned; Attila, subdued by the presence of Leo, chose to spare Rome. What words were exchanged remains a matter shrouded in the mystique of history. Some chroniclers postulate that Leo invoked the divine threat of Saint Peter and Saint Paul to dissuade Attila. Others suggest that the pope's serene demeanor and moral authority held sway over the barbarian king.

This moment of confrontation was both a test of Leo's diplomatic prowess and an assertion of the Church's growing influence. It demonstrated that where mortal might and imperial legions faltered, spiritual authority could prevail. The act of negotiating with Attila exemplifies Leo's remarkable ability to wield the power of faith against the forces of fear and destruction.

Indeed, the outcome was nothing short of miraculous to the Romans. Attila, who had previously razed cities and kingdoms, retreated from Rome's gates without a single battle. This act, attributed to Leo's intervention, reverberated through the epochs, as an emblem of divine intervention and moral victory. Leo's diplomacy here extended beyond mere political maneuvering; it was sacrosanct, leaving an indelible mark on the fabric of Christendom.

We must consider this episode as a luminous example of how ecclesiastical authority could mediate in worldly affairs with divine sanction. Pope Leo, through sagacity and an immutable resilience, proved that spiritual leadership could serve as the bulwark, protecting not just the soul, but the body politic. His encounter with Attila stands as a testament to his diplomatic acumen, an enduring symbol of how the will of the Church could alter the course of history.

Moreover, this negotiation underscored the transformative power of faith-led diplomacy. It showcased the extent to which an individual, armed with unassailable faith and the mantle of spiritual gravitas, could influence even the most formidable adversary. Leo's negotiation with Attila confronts us with a poignant reflection: the convergence of divine providence and human agency in the theater of history.

In the wake of this encounter, Pope Leo's stature grew not only among his contemporaries but also reverberated through the succeeding generations. The act of sparing Rome fortified the papal position within both ecclesiastical and secular spheres. Leo's legacy, thus, became intertwined with the concept of the papal protectorate—a role that would persist and evolve through the centuries.

Leo did not merely save a city; he saved a legacy, a faith, and a civilization. By drawing upon the strengths of his spiritual mandate, he engaged with the tumultuous world in a manner that exorcised the threats of his time. Leo's diplomacy was not built on the transactional politics of his contemporaries but on an unshakeable belief in the righteousness of his cause and the divine mission bestowed upon him.

In conclusion, "Negotiations with Attila the Hun" embodies more than a historical anomaly; it is the grand tableau wherein spiritual courage, moral certainty, and diplomatic genius coalesce. Pope Leo the Great, through this singular act, illuminated the incendiary path of the Huns not with swords, but with the sacred light of faith. Thus, he rendered a service not merely to his temporal contemporaries but to the enduring ethos of the Church and its divine guardianship over humanity.

Chapter 5: Ecclesiastical Reforms

In the hallowed annals of church history, Pope Leo the Great stands as a luminous beacon of ecclesiastical reform. Amidst tumult and discord, his resolute hand sought to fortify the very sinews of Christ's Holy Church. By adroitly strengthening the church's organization, he wove a tapestry of order where chaos once loomed. His vision imparted stern yet sagacious discipline, both to the clergy and the laity, thereby ensuring that sacred offices were manned by those imbued with devotion and integrity. These reforms, divinely inspired and meticulously implemented, were not mere edicts but rather the soul's clarion call to return to a purer, more sanctified practice of faith. Through these measures, Pope Leo the Great did not merely preserve the sanctity of the church; he emboldened its spiritual foundation, fostering a legacy that time's erosion could never diminish.

Strengthening Church Organization

In the fulness of time, the moment arose when the Church found herself in a need so dire that it compelled the most adroit and sagacious of leaders to fortify her very foundations. As the torrents of heresy and the sundry tumults of a decaying empire bore upon the ecclesiastical edifice, Pope Leo the Great saw fit to embolden the organizational sinews of the Church, ensuring it would stand unyielding against the buffetings of an apostate world. This undertaking, a veritable Herculean task, required a transcendence of mere administrative maneuvers; it was an endeavor wrought with keen theological insight and profound pastoral wisdom.

A firm ecclesiastical structure was not merely a matter of clerical logistics; it was, indeed, an embodiment of divine order, reflective of the heavens. Pope Leo set forth to delineate roles with such clarity that the harmonious function of the Church might mirror the celestial hierarchy. To him, bishops and priests were not simply managers of sacred rites; they were custodians of divine mysteries, whose authority must be recognized and revered. Thus, the hierarchy within the Church was defined with the precision of a sacred geometry, each role vital to the integrity of the whole.

In this sacred schema, Pope Leo reinforced the primacy of the Roman See, a bulwark against the rising tide of doctrinal confusion and schismatic fervor. The principate of Peter, upon whom the Church's foundation was laid, was not to be a mere historical relic but a living institution. By buttressing this primacy, Pope Leo ensured a central point of reference, a lighthouse amidst the tumultuous seas of theological discord and imperial decline.

This reassertion went hand in hand with efforts to consolidate the administrative functions of the Church. Diocesan boundaries were refined to foster closer oversight and ensure that the pastoral needs of the faithful were met with utmost diligence. The synodal system was revitalized, allowing for more frequent and meaningful episcopal gatherings, where pressing matters of doctrine, discipline, and liturgy could be discussed and resolved with the collective wisdom of the Church's leaders. These synods, part health-giving council, part fraternal covenant, fortified the unity and resolve of the clergy.

The appointment of capable and learned bishops was of paramount importance to Pope Leo. He understood that the staff shepherd must be sturdy and unwavering, for the shepherd's virtue or vice would ripple out to the flock. The Pope took pains to vet candidates, ensuring not only their theological acuity but also their moral rectitude. Such men of steadfast faith and unwavering integrity would be the bastions of orthodoxy, resilient against the encroachments of heretical thought and moral decay.

Moreover, a rigorous system of ecclesiastical courts was, under Pope Leo's stern yet sagacious eye, fine-tuned to maintain clerical discipline. Through these courts, disputes and transgressions were addressed with a judicious blend of mercy and firmness. No infraction was too minor, no misdeed too trivial—every act that threatened the fabric of the Church's sanctity was met with appropriate censure or penance. This judicious approach quelled potential discord and fostered a spirit of accountability among the clergy.

To ensure that the highest theological standards were upheld, Pope Leo emphasized the importance of clerical education. Seminaries and schools were invigorated, their curricula suffused with the studious rigor of patristic tradition and Holy Scripture. The clergy were not mere ritual functionaries; they were scholars, teachers, and preachers, equipped with the knowledge needed to guide the lay faithful and counter heretical propagations. By investing in the intellectual formation of the clergy, the Pope wielded knowledge as an invincible shield against ignorance and error.

Yet, it was not by firmness alone that Pope Leo sought to strengthen the Church organization, but also through the fostering of a pastoral spirit. The bishops and priests were called not only to rule but to serve; to be shepherds of souls imbued with the love of Christ, vigilant and tireless in their efforts to nurture the spiritual well-being of their flock. By emphasizing pastoral care, Pope Leo ensured that the Church's governance was tempered with compassion, mirroring the pastoral heart of the Savior.

His reforms extended into the realm of liturgical practice, where the order and sanctity of worship served as a reflection of the divine order. Standardizing liturgical texts and practices across various dioceses ensured that the Church's worship was uniform and reverent, elevating the minds and hearts of the faithful to the contemplation of the divine mysteries. Liturgical unity served as a potent symbol of the ecclesiastical unity Pope Leo so fervently advocated.

As the empire around them crumbled, Pope Leo's vision for a resilient Church organization provided not merely a bastion against external threats but a moral and spiritual sanctuary. The strength of the Church's organization, meticulously fortified under his keenly observant eye, bore witness to the resilience of faith amidst the ruins of secular power. His efforts to consolidate and enhance ecclesiastical structure laid the groundwork for a Church that could outlast kings and empires, standing as an enduring witness to the divine truth.

To wit, the influence of Pope Leo's ecclesiastical reforms resonated beyond his own epoch, echoing through the annals of history as a beacon of wise governance. The strengthened Church organization he bequeathed to posterity was not merely a transient institution but a pillar of divine governance that would underpin the Church's mission for centuries to come. The providential blend of authority and humility, of governance and service, defined the Church's role as both a temporal institution and a manifestation of the eternal kingdom.

Thus, in the fortification of the Church's organizational sinews, Pope Leo the Great did more than respond to the needs of his time; he wove a tapestry of divine order that would outlast the vagaries of earthly dominions. His sagacity and pastoral fervor combined to forge a legacy that would anchor the Church, ensuring her resilience and fidelity to the mission entrusted by Christ. This grand vision of ecclesiastical fortitude, rooted in theological profundity and pastoral care, continues to inspire and guide the Church through the vicissitudes of history, affirming the timeless truth that the gates of Hades shall not prevail against her.

Initiatives to Discipline Clergy and Laity

The sanctity of the Church hinges not solely on its celestial doctrines but equally on the terrestrial conduct of its stewards, both clergy and laity. Pope Leo the Great, in his pursuit of ecclesiastical purity, embarked upon numerous initiatives to discipline those within the fold, striving to mold both shepherds and flock in the illustrious image of Christ's virtue. The reforms he instituted were not merely edicts to be followed, but mandates to be lived, encompassing a radical transformation of moral and spiritual discipline.

Pope Leo envisioned a clergy deeply rooted in the virtues of humility, piety, and service. To this end, he established stringent regulations aimed at purifying the ranks of the clergy. Clerical celibacy, a principle staunchly advocated by Leo, was reinforced with uncompromising rigor. He perceived this vow not as a mere formality but as an embodiment of the clerical commitment to divine service, unmarred by earthly distractions. Failure to uphold this vow invited stern censure, a testament to Leo's unwavering resolve.

The laity, too, were not exempt from the Great Pope's disciplinary measures. Recognizing that the Church's moral fiber extended beyond the sanctuary, Leo promulgated decrees that sought to integrate the divine into everyday existence. He exhorted the laity to engage in acts of charity, maintain the sanctity of marriage, and uphold ethical integrity in all facets of life. Under his governance, the line separating the sacred and the secular grew increasingly permeable, with ecclesiastical virtues permeating the mundane.

In addressing the wayward clergy, Pope Leo employed an approach that melded compassion with firm rectitude. He emphasized the importance of pastoral care, mentoring errant priests back to the path of righteousness rather than casting them aside. For those irredeemably entrenched in transgression, Leo was unflinching in his imposition of canonical penalties, ensuring that the sanctity of holy orders remained unblemished. Such measures were not punitive for their own sake but were rather intended to preserve the sanctity of the sacrament and the integrity of the ecclesiastical institution.

A pivotal element of Leo's disciplinary initiatives was the establishment of councils and synods. These assemblies served as forums for the enforcement of ecclesiastical law and the adjudication of clerical misconduct. Decisions rendered in these councils were binding, underscoring the seriousness with which Leo approached ecclesiastical discipline. The decrees issued therein were documented and disseminated, ensuring uniformity in their implementation across Christendom.

Theological education was also prioritized as a means of fostering a disciplined clergy. Pope Leo instituted rigorous scholastic programs designed to inculcate doctrinal orthodoxy and ethical conduct within the ranks of the clergy. Seminary education under his aegis became a crucible for spiritual and intellectual refinement, producing clerics who were as learned as they were virtuous. This focus on education reflected Leo's belief that ignorance was a fertile ground for moral decay, and that a well-instructed clergy was less likely to stray from the path of righteousness.

Furthermore, Pope Leo addressed financial impropriety with strict regulations. He mandated transparent accounting practices and implemented checks to curtail embezzlement and corruption. The wealth of the Church, in Leo's view, was meant to serve the poor and needy, a sentiment echoed in his numerous homoies. Any deviation from this divine purpose was met with swift correction, ensuring that the Church's resources were used as a beacon of compassion and charity.

Amongst the sweeping reforms, Pope Leo's pastoral letters played a crucial role in instilling discipline. These letters, articulate and profound, served as moral compasses for both clergy and laity, delineating the virtues to be upheld and the vices to be eschewed. His exhortations, laced with theological profundity, were not mere rebukes but were instead aimed at nurturing the soul towards sanctity. He wielded his pen with the precision of a surgeon, excising moral rot and fostering spiritual regeneration.

Moreover, the penitential system under Pope Leo saw significant augmentation. Sinners were provided structured penitential regimens, tailored to the nature and gravity of their transgressions. This system was not designed to punish but to purify, offering a means to reconcile with the divine. The emphasis on confession and penance underscored Leo's belief in the redemptive power of divine grace and the transformative potential of sincere repentance.

In regions plagued by heretical influences, Pope Leo's discipline measures were particularly forceful. He dispatched emissaries to such regions, armed with both doctrinal knowledge and disciplinary authority. Their mission was dual—to root out heretical teachings and to reinforce ecclesiastical discipline amongst the clergy. These emissaries acted as Leo's vigilant eyes, ensuring that the purity of orthodoxy was maintained and that clerical conduct remained beyond reproach.

The innovative approach adopted by Pope Leo extended to the conflation of monastic and clerical life. By encouraging clerics to embrace ascetic practices typical of monasticism, he sought to elevate their spirituality and moral discipline. This integration infused the clerical community with a renewed sense of devotion and austerity, qualities that were expected to cascade down to the laity, elevating the collective spiritual consciousness of the Church.

Often overlooked but profoundly impactful was Leo's reform of liturgical practices. By standardizing and infusing greater reverence into the liturgy, he sought to reinforce the sacredness of worship. A disciplined liturgical life was, in Leo's view, a reflection of inner piety and a deterrent against moral laxity. The laity, observing and participating in such solemn rites, were subtly encouraged to mirror this disciplined reverence in their daily lives.

Pope Leo's reformative zeal did not shy away from confronting entrenched traditions and practices that were antithetical to Christian teachings. Pagan customs and superstitions, still lingering in various communities, were vehemently opposed. Through edicts and sermons, he sought to extricate these remnants of heathenism, replacing them with practices that were unequivocally Christian and morally edifying.

The unprecedented breadth and depth of Pope Leo's disciplinary initiatives were not without resistance. Yet, ever the astute diplomat, Leo navigated these challenges with a blend of firmness and conciliatory wisdom. His ability to weave doctrinal authority with empathetic pastoral care enabled him to enforce reforms without fracturing the ecclesial unity he so fervently cherished.

Indeed, the ecclesiastical reforms spearheaded by Pope Leo transcended mere administrative adjustments—they were a call to authentic Christian living. By disciplining the clergy and guiding the laity towards a higher moral ethos, Leo sought to create a Church that was not only divinely sanctioned but also visibly sanctified. His legacy, inscribing these reforms in the annals of ecclesiastical history, remains a testament to his unwavering devotion to the sanctity of the Church and the souls within its embrace.

Chapter 6: Social and Cultural Impact

Pope Leo the Great, in his unparalleled wisdom and sanctity, wielded an influence transcending mere ecclesiastical boundaries, permeating the very fabric of Roman society. Through his eloquent oratory and steadfast resolve, he championed the moral and spiritual renewal of the populace, exhorting them to aspire toward the divine. His sermons, suffused with ardent conviction, not only fortified the faithful but also served as beacons, illuminating the path of righteousness amidst the prevailing decadence. Moreover, Pope Leo's patronage of Christian art and literature fostered a renaissance of sacred creativity, inspiring the composition of hallowed texts and the adornment of sanctuaries with resplendent iconography. Thus, his impact was not confined to the sanctuary but radiated through the alleys of Rome, leaving an indelible mark on the cultural edifice of his era.

Pope Leo's Influence on Roman Society

Pope Leo the Great, a figure whose grandeur and piety enveloped the Roman society, stood as a beacon of spiritual fortitude. His influence rippled through the layers of the populace, extending beyond the confines of ecclesiastical walls, permeating the hearts and minds of the Roman citizenry. In a time when the Roman Empire teetered on the precipice of collapse, his leadership provided not only spiritual guidance but also a stabilizing presence that conferred a semblance of order and unity.

In the realm of social order, Pope Leo's impact was profound. His assertive actions in defending the city from the throes of external threats such as the imminent danger posed by Attila the Hun left an indelible mark on the collective consciousness of the Roman people. By confronting the peril head-on, he not only protected the physical sanctity of Rome but also reinforced the role of the papacy as a bulwark against chaos. This dual role of spiritual leader and temporal protector nurtured a sense of security and faith in the papal authority.

The societal influence extended further into the everyday lives of the Romans. Pope Leo's sermons and public discourses were not mere words; they were powerful currents that shaped the moral and ethical framework of the society. His teachings, grounded in Christian doctrine, exhorted the people to adhere to virtues of humility, charity, and righteousness. By constantly addressing the moral decay and providing a robust ethical model, Leo endeavored to mold a society that was not only religiously devout but also morally upright.

While Pope Leo's influence was evident in the public sphere, its depths reached the individual souls of the faithful. His exhortations in matters of faith and daily living encouraged a personal transformation that contributed to a broader cultural renewal. The emphasis on penance, repentance, and the pursuit of spiritual purity resonated deeply, fostering a community that was spiritually resilient and ethically conscious.

Moreover, Pope Leo's contributions to liturgical practices cannot be overlooked when considering his societal impact. By advocating for more structured and solemn liturgical ceremonies, he instilled a heightened sense of reverence and devotion amongst the people. The enriched liturgical life provided the faithful with a more profound spiritual experience, knitting them closer together in a shared sacred journey.

His theological stances also reverberated through the social fabric of Rome. The defense against heresies, most notably his actions against the heretical teachings of Eutyches, not only safeguarded the doctrinal purity of the Church but also upheld the unity of the Christian community. By quelling these doctrinal schisms, Pope Leo maintained a cohesive and unified front, which was crucial in a period marred by political fragmentation and social disarray.

The establishment of strong church organization under Pope Leo's aegis provided a framework that supported the social and cultural life of Rome. The initiatives to discipline both clergy and laity established standards that reinforced the moral and administrative efficacy of the Church. These reforms ensured that the ecclesiastical body functioned with greater integrity and efficiency, thereby enhancing its role as a stabilizing force in society.

In the domain of education and the preservation of knowledge, Pope Leo's influence was significant. He championed the clerical education, emphasizing the need for a learned clergy who could guide the flock with wisdom and prudence. This emphasis on knowledge not only elevated the spiritual leadership but also contributed to the cultural and intellectual enrichment of the society.

As a patron of Christian art and literature, Pope Leo set into motion cultural currents that left a lasting legacy. The flourishing of Christian artistic expressions during his pontificate reflected the deep intertwinement of faith and culture. These cultural undertakings not only beautified the sacred spaces but also stirred the aesthetic sensibilities of the people, engendering a culture that celebrated both divinity and human creativity.

His influence was also palpable in the domain of charity and social services. By promoting and supporting charitable activities, Pope Leo ensured that the more vulnerable sections of society were cared for. This compassionate approach not only alleviated immediate suffering but also fostered a communal spirit centered on the Christian principle of loving one's neighbor.

In essence, Pope Leo the Great's influence on Roman society was multifaceted, touching upon varied aspects of social, moral, intellectual, and cultural life. His leadership, grounded in unwavering faith and boundless wisdom, provided a moral compass during tumultuous times and carved a legacy that endured well beyond his earthly tenure. The transformation he wrought in Roman society was not merely a sweeping change but a profound and lasting renewal, deepening the adhesion to Christian values and enriching the Roman cultural landscape.

Thus, the era of Pope Leo stands as a testament to the enduring power of steadfast spiritual leadership in shaping the soul of a society. His legacy, imprinted upon the Roman ethos, was one of moral rectitude, cultural patronage, and compassionate governance, where faith served as the cornerstone for both individual and collective existence. The beacon of his influence continues to illuminate the annals of history, a guiding star for the faithful and a wellspring of inspiration for generations to come.

Contributions to Christian Art and Literature

Pope Leo the Great, a luminary of the early Christian era, left an indelible mark upon both the sacred art and literature of Christendom. His profound impact on these realms commenced with the theological gravity and eloquence of his writings, which served not merely as a voice of doctrinal authority but also as a rich tapestry interwoven with vibrant imagery and doctrinal clarity.

In a time when the visual arts were wielded as tools for religious instruction and devotion, Pope Leo accentuated the importance of iconography in rendering the divine mysteries accessible to the faithful. Engaging artisans and sculptors, he encouraged the creation of respectful and theologically accurate representations, urging that these works serve as more than mere aesthetic objects but as conduits of divine truth. His influence ensured that Christian art evolved from simple symbolism to intricate and grandeur forms, laden with profound spiritual significance.

Moreover, Pope Leo's sermons and letters, resplendent with stylistic grace and theological depth, became seminal texts that spurred the cultivation of a Christian literary tradition. His compositions, bathed in the luminosity of divine inspiration, were not mere declarations of faith but also masterpieces of rhetoric, embodying a synthesis of scriptural exegesis and pastoral care. They laid a foundation for the subsequent centuries of Christian literature, guiding and shaping the literary pursuits of theologians, bishops, and laypersons alike.

In his epistolary works, Pope Leo demonstrated an unparalleled adeptness at addressing diverse audiences—from unlettered peasants to erudite clerics and emperors—through language that resonated with each group in its own way. His eloquence in these letters was infused with a potent combination of simplicity and sophistication, ensuring his message was both comprehensible and profound. These letters helped to solidify Church doctrine, clarify theological controversies, and provide spiritual nourishment to the burgeoning Christian communities.

The festal epistles, in particular, encapsulate his contributions to Christian literature. Composed to address the faithful during key liturgical seasons, they are a remarkable collision of pastoral guidance and theological insight. These writings were not merely instructive; they were transformative, aiming to elevate the moral and spiritual lives of the faithful, urging holiness and unwavering faith amidst the tumultuous times.

Distinctly, Pope Leo encouraged the transcription and preservation of ancient Christian texts, understanding the power of written word in safeguarding the faith against the erosion of time and heresy. In this regard, his contributions extended into the realm of literary preservation, ensuring that the wisdom of the Church Fathers and early Christian thinkers was not lost but instead perpetuated and built upon by successive generations.

Among his most significant literary contributions, the Tome of Leo stands paramount. This letter, addressed to the Council of Chalcedon, is an exemplar of doctrinal clarity and rhetorical brilliance. It elucidated the nature of Christ in a manner both profound and accessible, thus playing a pivotal role in the Christological controversies of the time. The Tome's acceptance at the Council as a foundational text underscores its lasting import within Christian theological discourse.

The canonization of sacred music further illustrates Pope Leo's influence on Christian art. He saw the potency of hymns and chants in stirring the hearts of the faithful towards devotion. His endeavors included the encouragement of sacred compositions that echoed the holy scriptures and Church doctrines, thus infusing the liturgical atmosphere with a sense of the divine. These compositions were designed not just to please the ear but to uplift the soul, transforming ordinary moments into encounters with the sacred.

It would not suffice to speak of Pope Leo's contributions to Christian art and literature without mentioning his engagement with the construction of basilicas and churches. Understanding that these sacred spaces were extensions of theological truth and community life, he oversaw the embellishment of edifices that served as both places of worship and manifestations of the heavenly Jerusalem. These structures, adorned with mosaics, frescoes, and sacred art, bore the theological imprints of his vision.

Within these hallowed walls, the intermingling of art and liturgy reached an apotheosis. They became the vessels through which the faithful could visually encounter the mysteries of faith—each artistic detail a catechism in color and form, each stone and brushstroke a testament to divine beauty. Herein lay Pope Leo's legacy: the sacred as visible, the divine as palpable, through the very medium of human craftsmanship inspired by heavenly vision.

Thus, it can be concluded that Pope Leo the Great's contributions to Christian art and literature constituted a pivotal amalgamation of theological guidance and artistic inspiration. His efforts did not merely produce beautiful works and profound texts; they engendered a living tradition that continues to resonate through the ages. His legacy in these realms underscores a faith that is both doctrinally robust and aesthetically sublime—an enduring testimony to the sanctification of art and the illumination of the word.

Chapter 7: Pope Leo I's Sermons and Writings

Pope Leo I, known for his eloquent oratory and prolific writings, wielded the pen and pulpit with unparalleled mastery. His sermons, imbued with a philosophical depth that touched upon the divine mysteries, were not merely orations but instruments of spiritual transformation. Through his writings, Leo meticulously articulated the doctrines of the faith, combating heresies and elucidating the truths of Christian orthodoxy. The resonance of his teachings was profound, each word a clarion call to piety and steadfastness in a time of great religious tumult. His exhortations, delivered with dramatic fervor and theological precision, left an indelible mark on the hearts and minds of the faithful. Thus, the enduring impact of Pope Leo's sermons and writings continues to echo through the corridors of ecclesiastical history, bearing witness to his legacy as both a shepherd of souls and a guardian of truth.

Key Themes in Pope Leo I's Teachings

Pope Leo I, known as Leo the Great, stands as a towering figure, casting his philosophical and theological shadows far and wide. His sermons and writings embody a conflation of divine insight and ecclesiastical wisdom, weaving together the virtues of faith and reason. Of the myriad of themes present in his corpus, several pivotal motifs pervade his teachings, providing not only theological grounding but also a compass guiding the hearts and minds of the faithful.

Central to Pope Leo's teachings is the theme of **the Incarnation of Christ**. Leo's eloquence burgeoned in elucidation of the mystery of Christ's dual nature—both fully God and fully man. Emphasizing the hypostatic union, he offered an unwavering testament to the divine confluence in the person of Jesus Christ. This theological cornerstone served to counter various heresies of the time, thus bolstering Christological orthodoxy and ensuring the unity of belief amid doctrinal dissent.

Another salient theme in Leo's writings is the **primacy and unity of the Church**. He vehemently argued that the Church serves as the sole custodian of divine truth, vested with apostolic authority that descends directly from St. Peter. In this light, Pope Leo underscored the papal authority, highlighting its role as both the spiritual and administrative keystone of Christian unity. His efforts to consolidate ecclesiastical structure reverberate through the annals of Church history, providing a blueprint for harmonious governance.

Courage and moral fortitude resonate profoundly in Leo's discourses. He extolled the virtues of steadfastness and resilience, especially in the face of adversity. His homilies often conjured the specter of moral decay, urging the faithful to embody virtues that would fortify their spiritual resolve. With poetic fervor, he invoked the saints and martyrs, portraying their unyielding fidelity as exemplars for Christian conduct.

Pope Leo's teachings frequently explored the nature of **human sin and divine redemption**. He provided an acute understanding of mankind's fall from grace and the necessity of Christ's salvific sacrifice. Perhaps nowhere is this more evident than in his Lenten sermons, where he meticulously dissected the gravitas of original sin and the imperative for repentance. He posited that spiritual renewal and reconciliation with God are eternally accessible through the redemptive power of Christ's atonement.

Though divinely inspired, Leo was no stranger to the temporal realm. His writings also reflect the theme of **Christian charity and social justice**. He invoked the example of the Good Samaritan, compelling believers to extend compassion and aid to the less fortunate. His epistles often addressed the socioeconomic disparities of the time, urging the Church to act as the conscience of society, advocating for justice and mercy.

Furthermore, the theme of *spiritual warfare* looms large in Leo's rhetoric. He vividly described the Christian life as a militancy against the wiles of the devil. His images of the spiritual battlefield, replete with armor of faith and sword of righteousness, served to remind the faithful of their constant struggle against evil. Through vivid imagery and stirring exhortations, he rallied the Church as an army of virtue, poised to vanquish the forces of darkness.

The beatific vision of *eternal life and the Kingdom of Heaven* permeates Leo's teachings, offering comfort and hope to his flock. He painted celestial tableaux of the afterlife, extolling the eternal rewards that await those who endure in faith. These eschatological promises imbued his audiences with a sense of divine purpose, redirecting their temporal endeavors toward the celestial horizon.

Ecclesiastical humility and servitude resonate as bedrock principles in Leo's philosophy. He himself embodied these virtues, frequently identifying his papacy as a divine stewardship rather than a regal dominion. He humbly accepted the burdens and responsibilities of his office, ever mindful of his pastoral duty to serve the flock entrusted to him.

Finally, the motif of *doctrinal purity and vigilance* is omnipresent in Leo's works. He foresaw the dangers posed by doctrinal corruption and heretical teachings, advocating for a vigilant and proactive stance in safeguarding the Church's sacred traditions. His numerous encyclicals and pastoral letters aimed to rectify erroneous beliefs while nurturing the seeds of orthodoxy.

In summation, the key themes in Pope Leo's teachings intertwine like a grand tapestry, each thread contributing to the resplendent whole. His integration of Christological doctrine, ecclesiastical authority, moral virtue, social justice, and eschatological hope presents a comprehensive vision of Christian life. Such teachings continue to illuminate the path of faith, guiding countless souls toward spiritual fulfillment and divine communion.

Enduring Impact of Pope Leo's Writings

In the annals of ecclesiastical history, the writings of Pope Leo I stand as a formidable testament to the confluence of faith, intellect, and divine inspiration. His missives and sermons, teeming with theological profundities and pastoral wisdom, have long been revered, echoing through the corridors of time. The enduring impact of these works extends beyond mere parchment and ink; they encapsulate the very essence of Christian doctrine and fortify the foundation upon which the Church has been built. To fathom their influence is to traverse the epochs and perceive the ever-persistent resonance of his words in both sacred and secular realms.

Foremost among the writings of Pope Leo I are his influential *Sermones* and *Epistulae*. These compositions addressed the immediate needs of his flock, offering solace, guidance, and doctrinal clarity. His *Sermones*, in particular, became a cornerstone for liturgical preaching, advancing a scriptural exegesis that was both accessible to the layman and revered by theologians. With each homily, he laid down a mosaic of spiritual thought, meticulously crafted to uplift the human spirit and direct it towards divine truth. The meticulous blending of pastoral care and theological insight in these sermons has served as a model for generations of clerics.

Yet, it is in the realm of doctrinal development that Pope Leo's writings have cast the longest shadow. His *Tome of Leo*, drafted for the Council of Chalcedon, articulates the dual nature of Christ—an exposition that was critical in quelling the tumultuous waters of Christological heresies. The precision and clarity with which he expounded the doctrine of *hypostatic union* not only settled contemporary disputes but also cemented a doctrinal pillar that has weathered the storms of theological contention throughout the centuries. Leo's unwavering commitment to orthodoxy preserved the essence of Christian belief, safeguarding its integrity for posterity.

Moreover, the pope's letters and theological musings offer a vivid portrait of the socio-political landscape of his era. His engagements with secular authorities, his diplomatic negotiations, and his discernment in matters of faith provide an invaluable window into the interplay between church and state during the waning days of the Roman Empire. Through his correspondences, we glean insights into the tumultuous environment that shaped his pontificate, revealing the complexities and exigencies that informed his decisions.

Pope Leo's writings also laid the groundwork for subsequent ecclesiastical reforms. His keen awareness of the need for discipline among clergy and laity alike is evident in his pastoral letters, wherein he emphasized the sanctity of clerical conduct and the moral rectitude required of all Christians. These exhortations for a disciplined and devout clergy reverberated through the medieval Church, influencing the enactment of canonical decrees aimed at curbing laxity and corruption.

Further afield, the impact of Pope Leo's writings found fertile ground in the burgeoning realm of Christian literature and art. His vivid descriptions, metaphorical richness, and theological clarity inspired not only theologians but also artists and scribes. Manuscripts adorned with his sermons became treasures of monastic libraries, their illuminated margins bearing testament to the enduring appeal of his prose. The aesthetic and intellectual vigor encapsulated in his works stimulated a cross-pollination of ideas, catalyzing an enduring legacy that pervades Christian iconography and scholarly pursuits to this very day.

The ripples of Pope Leo's writings extend even to modern theological discourse, wherein his elucidations on core doctrines serve as touchstones for contemporary debate and reflection. Scholars delve into his texts, mining them for insights and reaffirming their relevance amidst the continually evolving landscape of theological thought. The pope's ability to straddle the realms of deep metaphysical reflection and practical pastoral care renders his works perpetually pertinent, a beacon of wisdom for those who seek to navigate the intricacies of faith.

In the domain of liturgical practice, the influence of Leo's sermons is indelibly etched. His emphasis on the importance of the liturgical calendar, the proper observance of feasts, and the sanctity of the Eucharist has imparted a lasting structure to Christian worship. The rhythms and cadences of his oratory continue to inspire homilists, ensuring that the spirit of his teachings finds voice in the ever-recurring cycles of the liturgy.

The aftermath of Pope Leo's death did little to dim the luminescence of his writings. Instead, they were meticulously preserved, studied, and disseminated by monastic communities and scholars. His works became essential texts within the corpus of patristic literature, their doctrinal soundness and pastoral sensitivity ensuring their primacy in theological education. Institutions of learning, both ancient and modern, have continuously sought to impart the wisdom enshrined in his texts to successive generations of theologians and clergy.

On another level, the enduring impact of Pope Leo's writings can be discerned in their role as instruments of unity and continuity within the Church. The pope's unyielding stance on doctrinal purity and his efforts to curb heresies fostered a sense of cohesion, reinforcing the Church's role as the custodian of divine truth. His writings served as a unifying force, bridging the temporal and spiritual realms and buttressing the continuity of Christian teaching from antiquity to the present day.

Notably, the influence of Pope Leo's writings transcends the confines of Christianity, touching even the broader framework of Western intellectual tradition. His engagements with philosophical constructs, his application of rhetorical techniques, and his integration of classical scholarship into theological discourse melded the sacred with the intellectual, thereby enriching the tapestry of Western thought. His writings represent a synthesis of faith and reason, a dialogue that has profoundly shaped the contours of Western intellectual heritage.

In conclusion, the enduring impact of Pope Leo I's writings is manifold and far-reaching, punctuating the spiritual and intellectual journey of the Church across the ages. His sermonic artistry, doctrinal elucidations, and pastoral exhortations constitute a reservoir of wisdom that continues to nourish souls and illuminate minds. Through the preservation and perennial study of his works, the legacy of Pope Leo the Great endures, a testament to the timeless relevance of his profound contributions to the Christian faith.

Chapter 8: Relations with Other Churches

As the ecclesiastical canopy extended further to the East and West, Pope Leo the Great found himself navigating turbulent waters with providence and wisdom unparalleled. He embraced the monumental task of unifying Christendom amidst an ever-widening chasm, wrought by theological disputes and cultural rifts. His correspondences sought to heal the breach between the Roman See and the Eastern Churches, with particularly keen focus on the controversies assailing the Councils and their doctrinal pronouncements. Leo's epistles, dripping with erudition and apostolic fervor, emphasized the oneness of the Church's corpus, grounding it in the immovable rock of Peter's confession. With meticulous care, he stitched the ecclesial fabric, his rhetoric both consoling and commanding. Through such sagacity, Pope Leo endeavored to bind the fractured limbs of the Body of Christ, ensuring that the faith of Nicene orthodoxy held steadfast against the tumultuous winds of heresy and discord.

Pope Leo I and the Eastern Churches

The era of Pope Leo I, illustriously known as Leo the Great, was marked by profound theological and ecclesiastical engagements with the Eastern Churches. This chapter endeavors to unravel the intricate tapestry of those interactions, a narrative interwoven with diplomacy, doctrinal clarifications, and unyielding defense of orthodoxy. The Eastern and Western branches of Christendom, though unified in faith, often found themselves at theological and political crossroads, where subtle differences had the potential to unravel the harmonious accord of the Universal Church.

Leo's ascension to the papacy in 440 A.D. came at a time when the Eastern Churches were wrestling with burgeoning heresies and theological disputes. One of the most significant confrontations was the Chalcedonian controversy, rooted in the nature of Christ. The East had been fraught with debates, especially surrounding the teachings of Eutyches, which birthed Monophysitism – the belief in Christ's single, divine nature, opposing the dual nature (divine and human) as accepted by the Church. Pope Leo's decisive intervention came through his renowned Tome of Leo, a letter to the Archbishop of Constantinople. This missive, rich in theological profundity, elucidated the Church's position on Christ's nature with unparalleled clarity and was a pivotal contribution to the Council of Chalcedon in 451 A.D.

Leo's theological acumen ensured that his teachings echoed throughout the Eastern Churches. The Tome of Leo was not merely a letter; it was a manifesto of orthodoxy that played a crucial role in the Council of Chalcedon. The council, convened with Emperor Marcian's approval, aimed to address the Christological controversies that threatened the unity of the Church. Leo's arguments were met with widespread acclaim, and his assertions were canonized in the Chalcedonian Definition, affirming the doctrine of the hypostatic union – Christ as one person in two natures, fully divine and fully human.

Yet, Leo's engagement with the East was not solely defined by theological discourse. He possessed an acute awareness of the broader political and ecclesiastical implications of his actions. His correspondence with Eastern patriarchs and emperors showcased his diplomatic dexterity, as he sought to maintain the integrity of the Church while navigating the intricate dynamics of power and influence. The Byzantine emperors, wielding substantial authority over ecclesiastical matters, often found themselves at odds with the papal stance. Leo's letters, therefore, were crafted with meticulous care, blending doctrinal firmness with diplomatic prudence.

However, the relationship between the papacy and the Eastern Churches was not devoid of tension. The controversy surrounding the Robber Council of Ephesus in 449 A.D. epitomized the fractious nature of their interactions. Convened by Emperor Theodosius II, the council aimed to exonerate Eutyches and affirm Monophysitism – a move staunchly opposed by Leo. The grim proceedings of the council, characterized by coercion and violence, were condemned by Leo as an orchestrated travesty, a perversion of ecclesiastical justice. His vehement opposition and subsequent efforts to nullify the council's decisions underscored his unwavering commitment to doctrinal purity and ecclesiastical integrity.

Leo's resilience bore fruit when the Council of Chalcedon annulled the decrees of the Robber Council, thereby reinforcing the Chalcedonian Definition. This triumph, however, did not signal an end to the discord with the East. The acceptance of Chalcedon was far from universal, with significant segments of the Eastern Churches, particularly in Egypt and Syria, rejecting its conclusions and adhering to Monophysitism. The seeds of schism were sown, and Leo's successors would continue to grapple with the repercussions of these doctrinal divides.

Furthermore, Leo's interactions with the Eastern Churches were emblematic of the evolving nature of papal primacy. The bishopric of Rome, bolstered by the legacy of Saints Peter and Paul, claimed a primacy of honor among the sees of Christendom. Leo, however, sought to fortify this primacy not merely as a matter of honor but of ecclesiastical authority. His assertions of papal supremacy, articulated through his correspondences and actions, laid the groundwork for the papacy's burgeoning role as the arbiter of orthodoxy and unity. The Eastern patriarchs, particularly in Constantinople, often viewed these claims with skepticism, wary of encroachments on their ecclesiastical sovereignty.

The doctrinal and jurisdictional tensions between the East and West, while ostensibly theological, were inextricably linked to the broader geopolitical landscape. The varying cultures, languages, and administrative structures of the Eastern and Western Roman Empires contributed to the growing sense of estrangement. Rome, with its Latin tradition, and Constantinople, steeped in Hellenistic heritage, represented two distinct civilizations within the Christian oecumene. Leo's efforts to bridge this divide were a testament to his vision of a united Christendom, yet they also highlighted the inherent challenges of maintaining unity amidst diversity.

Moreover, Leo's legacy in the Eastern Churches was cemented through his correspondence with key figures such as Patriarch Anatolius of Constantinople. Leo's letters, characterized by a blend of pastoral concern and doctrinal precision, revealed his deep investment in the spiritual well-being of the entire Church. His exhortations for unity and orthodoxy resonated beyond the confines of Rome, influencing theological discourse and ecclesiastical practices in the East. The enduring impact of his writings, particularly the Tome of Leo, continued to shape Christological debates long after his pontificate.

Despite the theological triumphs and diplomatic endeavors, the path to lasting unity with the Eastern Churches remained fraught with challenges. Theological disputes, particularly those surrounding Christology and the nature of the Holy Spirit, persisted, revealing the complex interplay of doctrinal fidelity and geopolitical exigencies. Leo's successors inherited a legacy of intricate relations with the East, navigating the delicate balance of asserting papal authority while fostering ecclesiastical harmony.

In conclusion, Pope Leo I's intricate dance with the Eastern Churches illustrates the multifaceted nature of his pontificate. His theological contributions, particularly through the Tome of Leo, were instrumental in shaping the Christological discourse of the time. Yet, his legacy extends beyond mere doctrinal expositions. Through his adept diplomacy, unwavering defense of orthodoxy, and efforts to assert papal primacy, Leo the Great left an indelible mark on the tapestry of East-West relations. His vision of a united Christendom, though challenged by the vicissitudes of history, remains a testament to his enduring impact on the annals of the Universal Church.

Efforts in Maintaining Church Unity

As the tumultuous seas of Christendom raged with theological discord and political upheaval, Pope Leo the Great embarked upon a mission that was both delicate and formidable: the preservation of ecclesiastical unity. The fabric of the Church, threatened by schisms and heresies, found in Leo a vigilant guardian who endeavored to weave its threads back into a seamless garment. His efforts were not merely acts of administrative acumen but bore the mark of a profound spiritual commitment to a unified Christian witness.

Leo's vision for unity demanded an emphasis on orthodoxy—right belief—as the cornerstone of the Church's integrity. To this end, Leo confronted numerous heretical movements with unyielding vigor. His famous Tome to Flavian, for instance, addressed the Christological controversies of the time, specifically the Eutychian heresy, asserting with clarity and theological precision the dual nature of Christ. This document not only found acceptance at the Council of Chalcedon but also became a pivotal reference for understanding the orthodox faith, exemplifying Leo's role as a bastion of doctrinal unity.

But it was not solely through the pen that Leo fortified the Church; his voice resounded across the ecclesiastical sphere. His sermons, imbued with scriptural wisdom and pastoral concern, urged the faithful towards a spirituality that transcended localised disputes. These homilies, reflecting the pulsations of his heart for a unified Church, exhorted believers to embrace a common faith and love, the twin pillars upon which the edifice of unity stood.

Indeed, Leo's efforts extended into the realm of diplomacy. His communication with Eastern Church leaders embodied the painstaking endeavor to navigate the complex waters of ecclesiastical relations. Leo's letters, many addressed to prominent bishops and emperors of the Eastern Roman Empire, reveal his nuanced approach: a blend of firm guidance and fraternal dialogue. By fostering respect and cooperation with the

Eastern Churches, Leo aspired to mitigate the divisive forces that threatened the Catholic fold.

The Council of Chalcedon remains one of the most significant indicators of Leo's commitment to unity. Although it did not resolve all theological disputes, it established a doctrinal coherence that undergirded ecclesiastical unity for generations. Leo's theological contributions at this council and his insistence on the primacy of the Roman See were not expressions of overbearing authority but rather instruments to harmonize the Church's doctrinal integrity.

Yet these grand efforts would have been incomplete without addressing the internal fractures within the Western Church. Leo turned his attention to various sects and schismatic groups, laboring tirelessly to integrate them back into the orthodox fold. Through pastoral letters and face-to-face encounters, he sought to bring back estranged members, urging them towards repentance, reconciliation, and reintegration, embodying the role of a shepherd ardently seeking his lost sheep.

Internally, Leo also knew that an undisciplined clergy could become the fissure through which division seeped. Hence, he instituted stringent ecclesiastical reforms aimed at enhancing clerical discipline and integrity. These reforms were not punitive measures but preventive ones, designed to foster a clerical class whose conduct and doctrine were above reproach, thus serving as exemplars of unity for the laity.

Perhaps one of his most profound contributions to unity was his articulation of the papal primacy. While this concept would later develop into a more centralized notion of papal authority, in Leo's time, it was a means to safeguard the Church against doctrinal fragmentation. By asserting the primacy of the Roman See, Leo argued for a focal point of unity, a singular ecclesiastical hub to which all could turn for doctrinal clarity and pastoral guidance.

Leo's correspondence was not limited to dogmatic or disciplinary concerns; it also reflected his pastoral heart. His letters often addressed the suffering and struggles of various Christian communities, extending support and solidarity. This was unity in praxis, a tangible representation of the Church as a single body, wherein the tribulations of one member were the concern of all.

In conclusion, the enduring legacy of Pope Leo's efforts in maintaining church unity is manifold. His theological acuity, pastoral sensitivity, and diplomatic finesse coalesced to create a bulwark against the forces of division. In the annals of ecclesiastical history, Leo stands as a testament to the power of dedicated and principled leadership, ever striving to maintain the unity of the spirit in the bond of peace.

Chapter 9: Liturgical Reforms and Innovations

In an epoch where the sacred rites of the Church required illumination and rivulets of divine grace, Pope Leo the Great instituted liturgical reforms suffused with both wisdom and innovation. Not content with the mere perpetuation of inherited customs, he sought to imbue the rituals with deeper theological resonance, punctuating each sacrament with doctrinal clarity. His liturgical innovations were manifold; they ushered in novel rites and profound traditions that echoed the perennial sanctity of Christian worship. The Creed, henceforth recited, became a bastion of orthodoxy, safeguarding the faithful from the capricious winds of heresy. With reverent precision, he refined the Eucharistic prayers, making them conduits of celestial grace. Verily, in his sacred stewardship, Pope Leo united the heavenly and earthly realms, bestowing upon the Church a liturgy that was as transcendent as it was immanent, enriching the souls of the congregants with divine luminescence.

Changes to Liturgical Practices Under Pope Leo

The epoch of Pope Leo the Great, a period brimming with ecclesiastical evolution, witnessed profound reforms in liturgical practices, deeds that would etch his name indelibly upon the annals of Holy Mother Church. In his wisdom, Pope Leo discerned that the fortification of the Church's spiritual life necessitated a liturgical revival, harmonizing the sacred rites with the theological profundities he so ardently defended.

Pope Leo sought to deepen the spiritual experience of the faithful, ushering an era wherein the sacred rites became more than mere ceremonial observances. He believed that a proper liturgy was a divine instrument to draw the congregation closer to God, engendering a sense of unity and purpose. Hence, he initiated changes that were as much an intellectual as a spiritual revival, aiming to synchronize the outward rites with the inward grace they symbolize.

The Mass, the centerpiece of Christian worship, saw notable refinements under Pope Leo's stewardship. He emphasized the Eucharistic celebration as a profound mystical participation in Christ's sacrifice. Leo's directives aimed to enhance the sanctity and solemnity of this central rite, inculcating a deeper reverence amongst the clergy and laity alike. By refining the language and gestures used during the Mass, he sought to elevate the minds and hearts of the faithful to the sublime mystery of the Incarnation and Redemption.

One significant change was the standardization of prayers recited during the Mass. He instituted a more uniform structure, which would not only mitigate regional liturgical inconsistencies but also foster a sense of universality within the Church. Pope Leo's modifications ensured that the prayers reflected the theological orthodoxy he so vigorously defended against heresies—a seamless tapestry, wherein doctrine and devotion were intertwined.

Furthermore, he introduced certain fixed elements within the liturgical calendar, thereby stabilizing the rhythm of Christian worship throughout the year. By reinforcing the commemoration of Christ's passion, resurrection, and the feast days of saints, Pope Leo sought to cultivate an ever-present awareness of divine mysteries in the lives of the believers. In his calculated wisdom, he perceived that a stable liturgical cycle could serve as a spiritual anchor amid the vicissitudes of temporal life.

Of noteworthy mention are the Prefaces—specific prayers recited during the Eucharistic prayer. Under Leo's insistence, these became more thematically rich, encapsulating the theological nuances of the feast or season they accompanied. His fluency in scripture and patristic teachings allowed him to craft these prayers with a philosophical depth that resonated profoundly within the liturgical framework.

In striving to amplify the majesty and splendor of the celebrations, Pope Leo placed great emphasis on the physical settings and the accoutrements used in worship. He advocated for the beautification of the altars and sanctuaries, directing that they be adorned in a manner befitting the divine mystery they hosted. The sanctuaries were not to be gaudy, but rather reflections of the heavenly glory, inspiring contemplation and reverence.

Pope Leo's reforms extended to the canonical hours, known collectively as the Divine Office, which structured the daily prayers of the clergy. This practice, encompassing Matins, Lauds, Prime, Terce, Sext, None, Vespers, and Compline, was standardized to maintain rhythm and order in the spiritual lives of the ordained. By stabilizing these hours, Leo ensured that the clergy's prayers resonated in unison, creating a symphony of intercession echoing throughout the Church universally.

In this endeavor, Pope Leo was meticulous about the role of music in the liturgy. Understanding its potent influence, he encouraged the use of chant—a mode of singing that could lift the soul closer to celestial harmonies. Gregorian Chant, though more closely associated with later developments, found its rudimentary encouragement in Leo's epoch. The use of chant served to unify the vocal prayers of the congregation with their meditative hearts.

The significance of these liturgical reforms extends beyond mere procedural adjustments. They were a means of re-invigorating the

Church's spiritual identity amid the socio-political tumult of the fifth century. The meticulous attention to liturgical propriety under Pope Leo's governance reflected his broader vision of a Church that stood as a bulwark of divine truth and human sanctity, even as the Roman Empire teetered on the brink of collapse.

In summary, the changes to liturgical practices under Pope Leo were profound and far-reaching. They weren't merely concerned with external observances but sought to enrich the internal spiritual lives of the faithful. By harmonizing the liturgical actions with doctrinal integrity and theological depth, Leo the Great bequeathed to the Church a legacy of worship that continues to inspire reverence, unity, and devotion. His reforms stand not merely as monuments of liturgical history but as living instruments of sacred tradition, ever relevant and sanctifying.

Introduction of New Rites and Traditions

The sacred chronicle of Pope Leo the Great is adorned with myriad episodes of pious innovation, a testament to his devotion to the spiritual refinement of the Holy Church. Amid the shadows of a waning empire, his sanctified hands wrought new rites and traditions that would resound through the annals of ecclesiastical history. These ceremonial innovations were not mere embellishments but theological proclamations, seeking to reflect the heavenly order within the terrestrial worship.

The introduction of these new rites invigorated the liturgical life of the Church, imbuing it with a renewed sense of sanctity and purpose. To discerning minds, the very essence of these rites revealed the profound theological insight and pastoral sensitivity of Pope Leo. He sought to elevate the hearts of the faithful towards divine mysteries, making the sacred rituals a conduit between the mortal and the eternal.

Among the most notable innovations were the enhanced liturgical celebrations of the feast days. The expanded observance of these days was not merely a calendrical adjustment but an invocation for the veneration of saints and martyrs, whose lives became parables of faith and constancy. The processions, litanies, and prayers instituted by Pope Leo brought a more profound communal spirit to these holy commemorations, fusing the Church's temporal journey with the eternal witness of the glorified saints.

The rites themselves were suffused with a dramatic interplay of word and gesture, sacrament and symbol. Pope Leo invested the Eucharistic celebration with a heightened sense of drama, mindful of its central place in the Christian faith. His reforms called for a more elaborate and theologically rich Eucharistic Prayer, accentuating the mystery of transubstantiation and the sacrificial love of Christ.

The integration of these new traditions fostered a deepening of communal participation. For instance, the inclusion of more congregational responses and the introduction of specific prayers for the laity during

Mass gave the faithful a more active role in the divine liturgy. This was not only an innovation in form but a pedagogical instrument, teaching the laity the intrinsic value of their participation within the mystical Body of Christ.

Leo's innovations also extended to the penitential practices of the Church. He was acutely aware of the need for rituals that could offer solace and repentance to a sin-stricken heart. In this spirit, he introduced new forms of the Sacrament of Penance, which included public penitential rites that underscored the communal aspect of sin and reconciliation. By placing greater emphasis on collective repentance and forgiveness, he sought to heal the wounds of both individuals and the broader community.

Moreover, the incorporation of these rites into the ecclesial life reflected Leo's strong pneumatological focus, emphasizing the Holy Spirit's active role in the sanctification process. New prayers invoking the Holy Spirit were inserted into the liturgical texts, seeking the Spirit's guidance and presence in the life of the Church. This pneumatological enrichment invigorated the spiritual dynamism of the Christian worship experience, making the liturgy a lively epic of divine-human interaction.

Pope Leo's reforms were not arbitrary impositions but were deeply rooted in scriptural exegesis and patristic tradition. Each new rite or modification bore the seal of biblical revelation and the wisdom of the Church Fathers. For example, the enrichment of the Easter Vigil and its attendant ceremonies was akin to an unfolding scriptural drama that invited the faithful to walk through the narrative of salvation history, from Creation through to the Resurrection.

In the sanctified silence of monasteries and the hallowed halls of basilicas, these treasured reforms resonated with the weight of theological profundity and liturgical elegance. As candles flickered and incense wafted through the aisles, the newly instituted rites transformed ordinary time into sacred time, inviting the worshippers to a deeper communion with the divine.

Beyond the confines of theology, the aesthetical beauty of these innovations served to elevate the senses. Art and architecture, music and vestments, all began to reflect the liturgical reforms initiated by Pope Leo. The visual splendor and acoustical majesty of the rites created an environment conducive to contemplating divine mysteries. Indeed, these tangible expressions of faith became windows to the ineffable, drawing souls into a closer embrace with the divine.

While these liturgical reforms were met with enthusiastic acceptance in many quarters, they also encountered resistance. Change, even when holy and inspired, often confronts the inertia of tradition and the reluctance of the status quo. Yet Pope Leo, with his theological acumen and pastoral wisdom, navigated these turbulent waters with a steadfast commitment to what he saw as the purer realization of the Church's vocation.

His resilience in the face of opposition is perhaps best exemplified by his measures in response to liturgical abuses and deviations. Striving for uniformity and reverence, Pope Leo confronted practices that threatened the sanctity and unity of the liturgy. His corrections were not merely punitive but aimed at restoring the integrity and clarity of worship, ensuring that the liturgical practices aligned with the doctrinal truths they intended to convey.

The introduction of new rites and traditions under Pope Leo was, in essence, a testament to his vision of a living, breathing Church—a Church ever-anchored in the apostolic faith yet dynamically engaged with the pastoral needs of the present. His liturgical reforms were a harmonious blend of venerable tradition and inspired innovation, beckoning the faithful to a deeper encounter with the divine mysteries.

As we contemplate the legacy of Pope Leo's liturgical innovations, we are invited to perceive them not merely as historical artifacts but as timeless conduits of divine grace. These rites, infused with the sacred wisdom of Pope Leo, continue to shape and nurture the spiritual life of the Church, guiding the faithful towards a more profound communion with the sacred.

Chapter 10: Education and Preservation of Knowledge

In the grand tapestry of his pontificate, Pope Leo the Great wielded the quill as mightily as the scepter, championing the illumination of minds and the sanctity of wisdom. His fervor for the enhancement of clerical education bore fruit through a rigorous dedication to scholarly revival, ensuring that the clergy were not merely stewards of faith but also venerable guardians of sagacity. The preservation of ancient texts, a paramount endeavor in his apostolic mission, stood as a bulwark against the relentless tides of oblivion. Leo perceived the sagas and scripts of antiquity as sacred vessels, teeming with divine and philosophical truths. Thus, his efforts were not confined to spiritual edification alone, but extended to the safeguarding of all knowledge, wielding it as a divine shield against the encroaching darkness of an era in turmoil. Pope Leo's endeavors in this realm immortalized him as a paragon of erudition, whose legacy in the preservation of knowledge has transcended the annals of time.

Enhancement of Clerical Education

The diversity and gravity of the times of Pope Leo the Great necessitated an undying devotion to the cultivation of intellect and spirit among the clergy. The enhancement of clerical education did not emerge from mere happenstance but as an edict woven with foresight and reverence unto the sacred texts. Leo the Great, sanctified by insight, perceived that the torch of faith could be handed down only through the edification of those chosen to be its bearers. Hence, noble efforts were embarked upon to refine and elevate the erudition of clergy members, knowing full well that their spiritual leadership would be the bulwark of Christendom.

One must consider the principles that undergirded this noble pursuit. Leo held fast to the conviction that rigorous study did not operate in isolation from spiritual growth. Nay, it was through diligent engagement with scripture and theology that the heart and mind of the clergy could align with the divine will. The balance between intellectual pursuit and spiritual devotion became a golden mean, wherein the scholastic endeavors were meticulously designed to parallel the profundities of faith.

Distinctly, the Holy Scriptures and Church Fathers' writings became cornerstones upon which the clerical education was established. Pope Leo fervently urged the clergy to immerse themselves in sacred texts, understanding them not solely as academic exercises but as divine revelations that mold the soul. Thus, the exegesis of Holy Writ, along with the rich commentary of church fathers, was paramount in the seminaries and learning halls of the time.

The word "catechesis" held profound significance under Leo's pontificate. The synthesis of doctrinal instruction and moral exhortation was not seen as mere pedagogy but as a transformative dialogue that conferred the sacred mysteries and truths of the faith unto the clergy. Leo's sermons themselves embodied this synthesis, providing a model of eloquence and theological depth that burgeoning clerics were to emulate.

Moreover, the philosophical traditions of the ancients, particularly the logical structures and rhetorical skills of Cicero and Plato, found a place within the ecclesiastical curriculum. Leo the Great displayed adept wisdom in recognizing that the ability to reason and argue persuasively was invaluable. Therefore, he ensured that clerics were well-versed in these classical disciplines, crafting eloquent orators and erudite defenders of the faith.

Pope Leo's vision extended beyond the local church to encompass a broader horizon of the Christendom. Unified by the doctrine, he propounded an ecclesiastical synergy where the educated clergy in variated dioceses could contribute to a coherent Church. The principles of scholasticism and conciliar deliberation found their roots in this enhanced clerical education, paving the way for the greater ecumenical dialogues that would emerge in later centuries.

In a world teetering on the brink of Roman decline, it is impressive to note Leo's strategies to fortify knowledge even amidst political chaos. Notwithstanding the looming perils, which included the invasions of barbarian hordes, Leo recognized that the preservation and enhancement of knowledge would be the Church's steady anchor. He worked ceaselessly to ensure that educational norms were maintained within monasteries and parochial schools, protecting them from the vortex of societal upheavals.

It would be remiss not to recognize the meticulous organizational skills that Leo the Great employed in establishing systems for the continuing education of clergy. Institutions under his influence were not confined merely to initial training but were envisioned as enduring centers for lifelong learning. In this, his endeavors presaged the very essence of universities that would flourish in the Middle Ages.

This enhancement of clerical education was not solely about intellectual rigor but also moral and ethical integrity. Indeed, Pope Leo was acutely aware that the priestly vocation was as much a testament of character as of knowledge. The rigorous curriculum went hand in hand with a profound discipline encouraging virtues such as humility, charity, and chastity. The education sought to sculpt not just scholars, but saints.

Leonine contributions to clerical education also underscored the importance of pastoral care and sensitivity. Clergy were taught that knowledge devoid of love was a clanging cymbal, thus emphasizing the application of their learning in the compassionate service to their flocks. The art of pastoral counseling, imbued with theological wisdom and human empathy, became a critical component of the clerical instruction.

Leo's efforts were not confined to the clergy alone. Recognizing the ripple effect that an educated clergy would have on the laity, he advocated for sermons and teaching that could edify the faithful. Through clergy who were well-educated and virtuous, the message of Christ reached the ears of the laypeople with clarity and authority, reinforcing the doctrinal cohesion of the Church.

The enhancement of clerical education thus had a ripple effect throughout the fabric of society. Well-formed clergy ensured that the teachings of Christ were not only preserved but also propagated with authenticity and fervor. The laity, through their pastors, could access the deep waters of theological and moral truths, building a robust and informed faith community.

Under Leo's direction, this perennial endeavor to better educate the clergy also served as a bulwark against heresies. Knowledgeable and vigilant priests became custodians of orthodoxy, equipped to recognize and refute erroneous teachings that threatened to erode the veritable foundation of the Church. The fortification of the mind likewise shielded the heart, guarding it against the insidious whispers of discord and falsehood.

It is perhaps through this undying commitment to the education of the clergy that Leo the Great's legacy endures most palpably. By laying down such stringent and sacred obligations upon the teachers of the faith, he ensured that the light of divine knowledge would not be extinguished by the tumult of earthly vicissitudes. Instead, it would burn ever brighter, through ages of enlightenment and darkness alike.

Indeed, this chapter in the grand narrative of Leo's accomplishments elucidates his grasp on the intrinsic connection between learnedness and spiritual fortitude. His work was not simply reformative but transformative, crafting a paradigm for clerical education that would echo through the corridors of the Church and into the annals of history. It was a testament to his profound understanding that only through the harmonious union of faith and reason, could the Church flourish as the unassailable beacon of truth and hope in a world ever in need.

In closing, the enhancement of clerical education under Leo the Great reflects a celestial harmony between wisdom and sanctity. It was an enterprise imbued with both urgency and reverence, guided by the conviction that those ordained to shepherd the faithful must carry within them the earnest knowledge of divine mysteries. Through his visionary efforts, Leo the Great ensured that the clergy would forever be prepared to nurture not only their own souls but also the souls of generations yet to come.

Efforts in Preserving Ancient Texts

In the grand pageant of history, the preservation of ancient texts assumes a role of monumental significance. Such efforts secure the wisdom of antiquity, rendering it imperishable against the ravages of time. Indeed, to Pope Leo the Great, the conservation of these venerable manuscripts was not a mere academic exercise; it was a divine mandate.

Amidst the profound theological discourses and ecclesiastical reforms of his pontificate, Pope Leo I was acutely aware of the fragile nature of knowledge. The drift of papyrus and parchment from one generation to the next was fraught with peril. Texts, imbued with the divine insights of the Church Fathers and Apostles, teetered on the brink of oblivion, threatened by the encroachment of barbarian hordes and the corrosion of age.

Pope Leo, perceiving the intrinsic value of these texts, summoned the Church to an unwavering commitment to their preservation. His approach was manifold: encouraging transcription, fostering monastic scholarship, and establishing ecclesiastical archives. Each measure bore testament to his profound reverence for the written word and his unwavering determination to safeguard it.

The monasteries, under his vigilant eye, became sanctuaries of learning and preservation. Monks, whose lives were a symphony of prayer and labor, were entrusted with the sacred duty of copying texts. Clad in the humble garb of their order, these scribes labored in dimly-lit scriptoriums, their quills dancing upon parchment, replicating the holy manuscripts with meticulous care. It was within these monastic walls that ancient knowledge found refuge, shielded from the vicissitudes of a shifting world.

Moreover, Pope Leo's initiative extended beyond mere transcription. He recognized the necessity of a centralized repository where these texts could be meticulously catalogued and accessed by the clergy and scholars. Thus, the establishment of ecclesiastical libraries became a focal point of his preservation efforts. These repositories were not merely for storage but were centers of study and interpretation, where texts could be examined, interpreted, and preached upon.

Pope Leo also championed the notion of clerical education that intertwined with the preservation efforts. By ensuring that the clergy were well-versed in the sacred texts, he created a culture of informed guardianship. The clergy, armed with knowledge and understanding, became the stewards of these ancient manuscripts, recognizing their significance and value.

The preservation of ancient texts was not without its challenges. The Church faced the constant threat of invasion and destruction. As hordes swept across the Roman territories, the risk of obliteration of these irreplaceable works loomed large. Pope Leo's diplomacy and political savvy became instrumental in protecting both the people and their cherished texts. His negotiations with marauding forces often included the plea for the safeguarding of sacred and cultural repositories.

Additionally, we must acknowledge the role of the faithful laity who, inspired by Pope Leo's example, often contributed to these preservation efforts. Wealthy benefactors provided the financial means for the transcription of manuscripts, the construction of libraries, and the support of monastic communities. Their devotion and generosity were indispensable to these endeavors.

The significance of preserving these ancient texts cannot be overstated. They were not mere artefacts of curiosity; they were vessels of divine wisdom, historical record, and theological insight. The writings of the Apostles, the Church Fathers, and early Christian scholars constituted the foundation upon which Christian doctrine was built. Their preservation ensured the continuity and orthodoxy of faith, guiding the Church through the tumultuous seas of heresy and schism.

As we reflect upon Pope Leo's efforts, it is clear that his dedication to preserving ancient texts was an integral part of his broader mission to fortify the Church. It was, in essence, a battle for the soul of Christian knowledge, a struggle to ensure that future generations would inherit the wisdom of their ancestors. Through his initiatives, Pope Leo I laid the groundwork for the Church's enduring legacy as a bastion of learning and scholarship.

In conclusion, Pope Leo the Great's efforts in preserving ancient texts were a testament to his profound understanding of the intrinsic value of knowledge. His multifaceted approach—combining transcription, education, and the establishment of ecclesiastical archives—ensured that the divine wisdom of antiquity would not be lost to the sands of time. Through his vision and dedication, the Church became a guardian of sacred knowledge, securing the legacy of Christian learning for future generations.

Chapter 11: Challenges and Controversies

The era of Pope Leo the Great was fraught with manifold tribulations and contentious disquiets, engendered both within the sanctum of the Church and the broader socio-political theatre. This intrepid Pontiff found himself besieged by internecine theological rifts, as heresies sought to rend the fabric of ecclesiastical unity. To fortify the Church's doctrinal moorings, Pope Leo wielded an authoritative pen, rendering judgments with the precision of a Roman jurist and the fervor of a divine oracle. Amid these ecclesial strivings, there burgeoned additional trials imposed by the waning Roman Empire's instability; vis-à-vis the Hun's formidable menace and the Vandals' rapacious onslaughts. Yet, with sagacious diplomacy and unwavering steadfastness, Pope Leo brokered peace where brute force faltered, thereby enacting a legacy of resilience and indomitable faith. Herein, emerged a shepherd whose confrontation with temporal powers did not merely shore the spiritual citadel but also cast his shadow upon the annals of history, enduring as a bulwark of moral fortitude and divine providence.

Internal Church Conflicts During Pope Leo's Pontificate

The annals of Pope Leo's pontificate are not unmarked by the strife and tumult that gnawed at the heart of the Church itself. In those times, not only the external forces and barbarian threats proved to be of concern, but also the internal dissentions that arose within the ecclesiastical body, testing the sanctity and unity of the Church. These conflicts, woven intricately into the fabric of Pope Leo's tenure, bore the gravitas of their time, showcasing the resolve and steadfastness of a pontiff committed to preserving the sanctity of Christian doctrine and the unity of the faith.

Foremost among these internal conflicts was the contentious issue of heresies that sprouted in various nooks and corners of Christendom. The specter of the Manichaean heresy loomed large, challenging the orthodox Christian teachings and spreading its tendrils into the spiritual life of the faithful. Pope Leo, recognizing the insidious nature of this heresy, marshaled his theological resources to counteract its influence, declaring ecclesiastical sanctions and disseminating sermons that elucidated the perils of such deviations from established doctrine.

Beyond heresy, the Church faced administrative and jurisdictional disputes that threatened its cohesion. Bishops and clerics often found themselves at loggerheads, their ambitions and interpretations leading to schisms that required the firm hand of the pontiff to reconcile. The case of Hilary of Arles, who resisted the limits imposed on his authority by the pope, demonstrated the delicate balance Leo had to maintain. Through diplomatic letters and authoritative decrees, Pope Leo reasserted the primacy of the Roman See, underscoring the hierarchical structure that was vital for maintaining order within the Church.

It was during this period that the subtle yet profound conflict of monastic practices emerged. The burgeoning monastic communities, with their varying interpretations of ascetic life, occasionally found themselves in doctrinal conflicts with the episcopal hierarchy. Pope Leo, himself a proponent of monastic discipline, took it upon himself to mediate in these disputes, guiding the monks towards a harmonious existence within the larger ecclesiastical framework. Through his exhortations and pastoral care, he fostered an environment where monastic zeal could flourish without undermining episcopal authority.

One cannot overlook the divisive Council of Chalcedon that took place during his pontificate. The council, with its declaration of the two natures of Christ in one person, was a watershed moment, yet it also sparked significant discord. Certain factions, unable to reconcile with the council's decrees, created fissures that reverberated across Christendom. Pope Leo, whose Tome was instrumental in the council's Christological definitions, faced the arduous task of enforcing the decrees while extending olive branches to dissenting groups. His epistles and diplomatic efforts reveal a pontiff deeply committed to unity, yet unwavering in doctrinal truths.

Clerical misconduct further compounded the internal conflicts within the Church. Pope Leo, with his unwavering sense of duty, sought to elevate the spiritual and moral standards of the clergy. Instances of moral laxity among priests were met with stringent corrective measures. His pastoral letters often bore witness to his insistence on clerical purity and devotion, as he sought to emulate the sanctity of the early Church fathers. Through synodal decrees and personal admonitions, he labored to bring errant clergy back into the fold, ensuring that the shepherds of the flock were themselves unwavering in their faith and conduct.

The dichotomy between the Western and Eastern Churches also cast a shadow over his pontificate. The theological and liturgical divergences, though not yet leading to a formal schism, necessitated vigilant negotiation and correspondence. Pope Leo's interactions with the Eastern bishops, marked by both cordiality and firmness, exhibit his dual approach of maintaining doctrinal purity while striving for ecclesiastical harmony. His letters to the patriarchs of Constantinople and the other Eastern sees reflect an era where every word and gesture carried immense weight, striving to bridge the theological divides that threatened the unity of Christendom.

Amid the lofty theological and administrative disputes, the internal conflicts during Pope Leo's reign extended to the laity's role within the Church. The burgeoning influence of lay leaders in ecclesiastical matters sometimes led to clashes with ordained authorities. Pope Leo, advocating for a clear demarcation between lay and clerical roles, issued decrees that sought to preserve the sanctity and hierarchy of Church governance. His actions underscored the belief that while the laity played a vital role in the life of the Church, the ultimate authority in spiritual matters rested with the ordained clergy.

Pope Leo's pontificate was thus a crucible in which the enduring strength of the Church was tested and refined. His ability to navigate these internal conflicts with theological acumen, pastoral sensitivity, and ecclesiastical authority revealed a pontiff singularly dedicated to the unity and sanctity of the Christian faith. These struggles, while fraught with tension and discord, ultimately underscored the resilience of the Church under his spiritual stewardship. The internal conflicts, myriad and complex, provide a testament to his unyielding commitment to preserving the integrity and unity of the Church amidst the vicissitudes of his time.

Reflecting upon these tumultuous years, one discerns a pope who faced not just the external barbarians but also the internal tempests with equal fortitude. He emerged not only as a theological luminary but also as a stalwart guardian of ecclesiastical unity. In his resolves and decisions, we find the echoes of an era that sculpted the very bedrock of Christian orthodoxy. Thus, the internal church conflicts during Pope Leo's pontificate bear witness to his profound influence on the enduring legacy of the Church, a legacy imbued with his wisdom, courage, and unshakable faith.

Political and Social Challenges Faced by Pope Leo

Amidst the grandeur and solemnity of ecclesiastical governance, there existed a turbulence of political and social adversity which Pope Leo, hailed as the Great, encountered with both fortitude and sagacity. The waning days of the Roman Empire presented an epoch of pervasive chaos, as barbarian invasions across Europe set ablaze the teetering dominions of Rome. Leo, in assuming the mantle of the Supreme Pontiff, found himself ensnared within the very maelstrom of such transformative, albeit tumultuous, times.

Imperial Rome, once a colossus bestriding the known world, found itself beleaguered by incessant incursions wrought by the Huns, Vandals, and other insurrective forces. These forays orchestrated by barbarian armies threatened not only the temporal stability of an empire but also the spiritual bastion under Leo's custodianship. The Roman Empire's authoritative grip slackened, fostering a vacuum teeming with discord and instability, a context within which Leo wielded his influence with measured prudence and unwavering resolve.

Leo's diplomacy shone forth with undeniable brilliance during his fabled encounter with Attila the Hun. It was a moment wherein the specter of annihilation loomed ominously over Rome. The Hunnic kingdom, under Attila's formidable leadership, had ravaged vast swathes of Europe, bringing even the stout hearts of seasoned Roman legions to tremor. Leo stood as the bulwark between civilization's precipice and complete ruination. His negotiation with Attila is documented as a masterstroke of divine guidance and rhetorical prowess, whereby the so-called "Scourge of God" was dissuaded from sacking Rome. This augments the narrative of Leo's perspicacity in political maneuvering amidst threats that were both corporeal and existential.

Yet, it was not merely the specter of external invaders that vexed Leo's pontificate. Intrigues and rivalries within the ecclesiastical framework further compounded his tribulations. The Eastern Church, with its centric political influences and doctrinal divergences, often found itself at odds with the primacy claimed by Rome. These conflicts, doctrinal and territorial, necessitated a pontiff of formidable intellect and unwavering dedication to the precepts ordained by the apostolic succession. Leo's endeavors to maintain ecclesiastical unity bore testament to a leadership that, even amidst crisis, sought congruity over discord.

The civil authority of Rome during this period, fragmented and languishing under the weight of barbaric onslaughts and internal decadence, often impeded the church's mission. The senate and magistratum, once paragons of Roman civility and law, had dwindled into inefficacy. Leo's pontificate bore the additional burden of navigating an administration that could no longer uphold its civic duties, thus compelling the church to assume a more pronounced role in governance and societal stewardship.

Moreover, Leo faced social challenges magnified by the socio-economic disparities that plagued a crumbling empire. The urban poor, destitute and forsaken by a failing civic structure, turned inexorably towards the church for succor. Displacement, famine, and poverty were rampant, and Leo's stewardship embodied the church's compassionate response. His sermons and initiatives underscored a divine mandate to care for the needy and uphold the sanctity of human dignity amidst a society beleaguered by despair and disorder.

The ecclesiastical reforms Leo instituted were not merely inspired by doctrinal purity but were imperative measures to counteract ecclesiastical corruption and venality, which had burgeoned amidst the flux of social upheaval. The restructuring of clerical discipline and the fortification of doctrinal orthodoxy under his guidance sought to restore the moral and spiritual integrity of the clergy, an endeavor assiduously pursued with a vision anchored in both pastoral care and principled governance.

Leo's written correspondences and sermonic discourses reveal the indelible imprint of a leader who, amidst ephemeral tribulations, sought to etch an eternal legacy of faith and reason. Through these documents, the vestiges of his thoughts reflect a world grappling with profound metamorphoses in the very fabric of its existence. His epistles, dispatched to various ecclesiastic and political figures, embody the intellectual diligence with which he addressed the manifold challenges of his time.

Pope Leo's interaction with the social fabric of Roman society was also characterized by his endeavors to integrate the disparate elements of Roman citizenry into a cohesive and harmonious body of Christ. He strove to mitigate the fractures precipitated by socioeconomic disparities, ethnic diversities, and cultural incongruities. This integration was emblematic of a church that, under Leo's stewardship, embraced not only the spiritual guidance of its flock but also their temporal well-being.

The socio-political landscape in which Leo operated was as much a testament to his resilience as to his astute understanding of governance. He recognized that the ecclesiastical sovereignty, within an imperium in decline, necessitated a symbiotic relationship with both the lay populace and aristocratic echelon. This adaptive governance is a profound reflection of his epoch's exigencies, demanding a pope who could deftly traverse the realms of spiritual and temporal leadership.

Pope Leo the Great, therefore, stands not merely as a theological luminary but as a harbinger of stability and moral rectitude within an era plagued by disarray. His navigation through the political and social maelstrom bears witness to a pontificate that was as resilient as it was enlightened, carving a path of righteousness and reason amidst the most harrowing adversities of his age.

Chapter 12: Legacy and Canonization

As the twilight of Pope Leo I's earthly tenure above unfurled and gave way to the immortal annals of history, his legacy stood etched, not in mere stones of a ruined Rome, but in the hearts and doctrines of Christendom. Forsooth, his theological acumen and indomitable spirit bore the weight of both ecclesiastical and temporal realms, their ripples felt unto the ends of Christ's domain. Through a path hallowed by trials, he emerged a beacon, imbuing the Church with enduring doctrines and fortifications against heresies untold. Upon his death, the mantle of sainthood was not lightly bestowed; it was wrought through venerable canonization processes, a divine affirmation of his sanctity and an eternal testament to his life's works. Thus, Saint Leo the Great ascended not only into Heaven's embrace but into the sacrosanct veneration of Holy Mother Church, his legacy a tapestry woven with threads of unwavering faith and ceaseless toil.

The End of Pope Leo I's Pontificate

The twilight of Pope Leo I's pontificate unfolded amidst the shadows of great turbulence and luminous clarity, woven together to shape a legacy that would reverberate through the annals of ecclesiastical history. As the 460s approached, the venerable Pope, whose steadfast resolve had already confronted manifold trials, found himself gazing upon an evolving tapestry of Christendom. His soul, weathered but unyielding, continued to steer the barque of Peter through tempestuous seas.

The breadth and depth of Pope Leo's spiritual vision could not be overstated. Even as age began to weigh upon his physical frame, his intellect and spiritual fervor remained undiminished. He interfaced with the pressing issues of his time with an astuteness that only deepened with years of service. The vigor with which he defended the orthodoxy, particularly against the Eutychian heresy, persisted until his final breaths, encapsulating the enduring essence of his theological combat.

In the final years of his pontificate, Pope Leo's efforts were markedly directed towards bolstering the structural integrity of the Church. This period saw significant reinforcement of the Petrine primacy, ensuring a solid foundation upon which the successors of Peter could continue to build. Leo's correspondence and formal ecclesiastical documents revealed a pontiff still profoundly engaged with both doctrinal precision and pastoral care. His doctrinal tenacity was not merely a matter of intellect but an existential fidelity to the divine mission bestowed upon him.

Despite the unceasing demands of his pontificate, Pope Leo did not eschew the contemplation of the divine mysteries and the welfare of the flock entrusted to him. His eloquent sermons and epistolary exchanges during these final years imparted solace and direction to the faithful. In these writings, one discerns a heart profoundly united with the divine, a shepherd whose voice echoed the call to eternal unity in Christ.

Amidst the rigors of ecclesiastical governance, Pope Leo also endured personal afflictions and declining health. His physical frailty became increasingly apparent, yet it was in this vulnerability that his spiritual strength shone most brilliantly. The pontiff's acceptance of suffering mirrored the passion of Christ, offering a poignant testimony of faith to a Church often beleaguered by external threats and internal discord.

The state of the Roman Empire, teetering on the brink of disintegration, further compounded Leo's responsibilities. As barbarian onslaughts loomed over the horizon, his resolute diplomacy and unyielding spirit remained pivotal in safeguarding Rome. The experiences etched in his soul since the fateful encounter with Attila the Hun and subsequent negotiations with other marauding leaders fortified Leo's resolve to protect the sanctity of the Eternal City.

Notwithstanding the ephemeral victories of his diplomatic engagements, Leo conscientiously prepared the Church to face the uncertain future that lay beyond his tenure. His foresight in ecclesiastical matters, particularly his insistence on doctrinal clarity and administrative reform, functioned as the bedrock for subsequent generations. These measures were aimed not merely at preservation, but at fostering the flourishing of the Christian faith amidst prevailing chaos.

In November of 461, as the autumn leaves began to fall upon the ancient capital, Pope Leo I took his final leave of this temporal world. His death signaled the end of an epoch, a culmination of a life rendered in service to God and His Church. Known as Leo the Great, the pontiff who had once stood undaunted before the terror of the Huns now stood before the heavenly tribunal, his past labors a veritable offering of devotion.

The solemnity of his passing brought forth an outpouring of veneration and sorrow from the faithful. Perhaps the most poignant testimony to his enduring influence was the immediate recognition of his sanctity and the commencement of processes that would lead to his canonization. His burial in the basilica of St. Peter cemented his eternal association with the apostle whose mantle he had so ardently championed.

The conclusion of Pope Leo I's pontificate did not denote a cessation of his influence. Rather, it marked the beginning of an enduring legacy that would inform and inspire the Church in the centuries to follow. His writings continued to be a wellspring of theological riches. His example of pastoral courage provided a model for all who would shepherd God's people in times of peril and peace alike. The indomitable spirit and unwavering faith of Pope Leo I consecrated his memory as both a beacon and bulwark of the Christian tradition.

As we reflect upon the terminal chapter of his earthly ministry, we discern in Pope Leo I an illustrious figure whose labors imparted profound ecclesiastical and theological advances. The end of his pontificate seamlessly wove into the greater narrative of the Church, embodying the eternal vigilance and transcendent hope to which Christendom aspires. And thus, in the pages of history, the final strokes of Leo's tenure painted a portrait not of conclusion but of everlasting significance, a pontificate that ceased in the temporal yet commenced anew in the celestial chorus of saints.

The Canonization Process and Pope Leo's Sainthood

As the twilight of Pope Leo the Great's life drew near, the Church mourned the imminent loss of a formidable shepherd whose wisdom and sanctity had guided the faithful through turbulent times. Yet, even as his final breath affirmed his mortal end, Pope Leo's legacy would endure, hallowed and immortalized through the holy rite of canonization. This process, meticulous and sacred, sought to affirm that Leo's virtues on Earth warranted veneration in Heaven.

The journey towards canonization is neither swift nor unilateral; rather, it involves a rigorous examination of the candidate's life, miracles, and virtues. The initial step in this hallowed process is the declaration of the individual's heroic virtue. Here, the Church scrutinizes the deeds, writings, and personal holiness of the deceased, seeking testimony that Christ's light shone luminously through their actions and teachings. For Pope Leo, his actions spoke volumes. His fervent defense against heresies and his profound development of Church doctrine proved to be pivotal in solidifying the faith of countless souls. Thus, his heroism in virtue was undoubtedly pronounced.

Once deemed to have lived a life of heroic virtue, the title of "Venerable" is bestowed upon the candidate. For Leo, this phase of veneration resonated deeply within the hearts of the faithful who had witnessed his unwavering leadership. The next step in his canonization was the verification of miracles attributed to his intercession. Miracles serve as divine affirmations, indisputable signs that the candidate's soul resides in heavenly glory. These phenomena are authenticated through stringent investigation, ensuring that their origin defies natural explanation and attributes solely to heavenly intervention.

Pope Leo's intercessory powers soon became evident through numerous accounts of miraculous healings and divine interventions. Among these, the testimony of a young woman, gravely ill and despaired of by physicians, stands out. She claimed to have beseeched Leo for aid, and upon invoking his holy name, she rose from her sickbed, rejuvenated and whole. Such wondrous occurrences were meticulously documented and presented as evidence of Leo's sanctity.

Upon validation of one miracle, Leo was beatified, earning the title "Blessed." However, sainthood requires further divine endorsement; hence, another miracle, post-beatification, was necessary. This second miracle arrived in the form of a ship caught in a perilous storm. The crew, facing imminent peril, invoked Leo's intercession, and the tempest miraculously abated, delivering the vessel safely ashore. This second testament fortified the Church's decision, and thus Leo ascended to the illustrious company of canonized saints.

The significance of Leo's canonization extends beyond mere recognition. It affirms the transcendental bridge between his ecclesial contributions and the spiritual welfare of the faithful. Pope Leo's sainthood serves as an eternal beacon, guiding the devout through the labyrinth of secular existence towards the celestial haven. Moreover, it underscores the Church's role as custodian of divine truth, reinforcing the sanctity of the papal office through exemplars of faith such as Leo.

In addition to miracles, the canonization process also pays homage to the theological and pastoral legacies left behind by the saint. Leo's treatises and sermons encapsulated a wellspring of doctrinal clarity and pastoral care. His "Tome of Leo," a paramount articulation of Christological orthodoxy, was not merely a scholarly treatise but a divine instrument preserving the true nature of Christ amidst doctrinal errancies.

His profound understanding and articulation of doctrine provided a rock upon which the Church stood firm against the waves of heresy. The Council of Chalcedon, where his "Tome" was read aloud and received with acclamation, stands as testament to his theological prowess and his unrelenting resolve in preserving the Deposit of Faith. Such profound contributions undoubtedly served as an anchor, affirming the Church's decision to elevate him to sainthood in recognition of his theological fortitude.

The sanctification of Pope Leo also illuminates the intrinsic value of leadership grounded in unwavering faith and dedicated service. His diplomatic engagements, such as his historic encounter with Attila the Hun, reflect a pope whose strategic acumen was tempered by spiritual insight. This encounter, marked not by martial conflict but by profound moral conviction and divine supplication, underscored his role as a divine emissary. This event enshrined in sacred memory, portrays Leo as a harbinger of divine peace, further substantiating his worthiness of sainthood.

Moreover, Leo's ecclesiastical reforms revealed a visionary leader whose mission extended beyond temporal governance to the spiritual edification of the Church's hierarchy and laity. His relentless efforts to discipline clergy and laity, his initiatives to strengthen church organization, and his profound understanding of pastoral care, forged a sanctified Church that mirrored the heavenly order. These reforms, intricately woven into the fabric of his legacy, imprinted upon the annals of ecclesiastical history, validated his eventual canonization.

Pope Leo's influence on Roman society and his contributions to Christian art and literature also played pivotal roles in underscoring his sainthood. Through his sermons, he not only addressed the spiritual needs of the Roman populace but also championed moral and social causes, advocating for the welfare of the poor and marginalized. His literary contributions, rich with theological depth and pastoral concern, continue to enlighten and inspire the faithful, further cementing his sanctity.

The collective memory of the Church, preserved through ages, rejoices at the sanctification of figures like Pope Leo. His canonization is more than a posthumous honor; it is an affirmation of divine favor and an eternal testament to the transformative power of faith. His elevation to sainthood inspires the faithful to emulate his virtues, to seek divine wisdom, and to uphold the sanctity of the Church in the face of worldly tribulations.

In summation, the canonization of Pope Leo the Great is a confluence of divine grace and ecclesial recognition. It affirms his earthly endeavors and divine intercessions as manifestations of sanctified living. His legacy, perpetuated through the reverence of his sanctity, continues to guide the faithful, a luminous star in the firmament of Church history, forever enshrined in both Heaven's glory and Earth's veneration.

Conclusion

In the annals of history, few figures shine as luminously as Pope Leo the Great. Through the span of his life and pontificate, his actions and teachings resound with an echo of divine wisdom and earthly sagacity. In the heart of a decaying Roman Empire, he stood firm as a bulwark of faith, a beacon to the beleaguered faithful, and a shepherd to his scattered flock. This narrative has journeyed through multifarious facets of his life and influence, yet it is here, in the solemnity of our conclusion, that we draw the final threads together.

Pope Leo's theological acumen was like an unassailable fortress, erected against the battering waves of heresy, especially the pernicious spread of Eutychianism and Nestorianism. His incisive mind and unwavering conviction steered the Church's doctrinal vessel through tempestuous seas. By reinforcing the duality of Christ's nature in the Tome of Leo and asserting theological clarity at the Council of Chalcedon, he fortified the bedrock upon which the edifice of Christian orthodoxy stands.

Beyond theology, his political and diplomatic dexterity was equally remarkable. It was no mere happenstance that he faced Attila the Hun—a moment etched in time, encapsulating the gravity of his peacemaking prowess. His discourse, though veiled in mystery, bore the fruits of averting Rome's imminent destruction. Such diplomacy was not confined to external threats alone; within the Church, he instituted reforms that imbued the ecclesiastical hierarchy with greater discipline and cohesion.

In societal spheres, Pope Leo's impact transcended mere religious doctrine. He was not only a spiritual leader but also a cultural and intellectual luminary. His sermons reverberated with moral edification and an eloquence that inspired literary and artistic endeavors. The cultural renaissance that sprouted under his aegis was both a preservation and an augmentation of Christian artistic and intellectual heritage, with tendrils that reached far into subsequent generations.

Yet, perhaps the most profound testament to his legacy lies in his sermons and writings. These enduring relics are more than just scholarly artifacts; they are living testaments to his unwavering faith and sagacity. Through these texts, the voice of Pope Leo continues to resonate, offering guidance, inspiration, and theological clarity to both clergy and laity alike.

Ecclesiastical unity was another pillar of his pontificate. His interactions with the Eastern Churches demonstrated a concerted effort to bridge divides and foster a unified Christendom. His meticulous correspondence and conciliatory overtures sought not the erasure of diversity but the embrace of unity in faith and doctrine. Despite the perennial schisms and tensions, his vision of unity offers a paradigmatic example of ecclesiastical diplomacy and fraternity.

In the realm of liturgical reforms, Pope Leo's contributions were transformative. His zealous pursuit of enhancing worship practices reflected a profound understanding of liturgy as the heartbeat of Christian life. Through the introduction of new rites and the refinement of existing traditions, he ensured that the sanctity and solemnity of divine worship were preserved and elevated. These reforms were not mere cosmetic changes but were imbued with a theological rigor that underscored the sacred mysteries of the faith.

The preservation of knowledge and the enhancement of clerical education under Pope Leo's guidance further underscored his intellectual leadership. At a time when the flame of classical wisdom flickered precariously, his efforts to safeguard ancient texts and elevate clerical learning served as a bulwark against the encroaching shadows of ignorance. His foresight in this regard cemented the Church's role as a custodian of knowledge and a beacon of enlightenment amidst the declining Roman world.

Pope Leo's pontificate was not without its challenges and controversies. Internal strife and external pressures tested the mettle of his leadership. Yet, in the crucible of adversity, his resolve was tempered and refined. His responses to these challenges—marked by prudence, fortitude, and faith— offer a poignant reflection of his enduring legacy.

The final chapter of Pope Leo's life saw the culmination of his earthly ministry and the commencement of his celestial legacy. The process of his canonization affirmed the sanctity and excellence of his life and works. As a Saint, Pope Leo the Great remains a towering figure whose influence transcends the temporal confines of his era, offering a source of inspiration and veneration to the faithful across the ages.

In summation, the life and legacy of Pope Leo the Great are a testament to the enduring power of faith, wisdom, and leadership. His contributions to theology, ecclesiastical organization, political diplomacy, societal influence, and intellectual preservation are immeasurable. As we close this narrative, it is fitting to regard Pope Leo not merely as a historical figure but as a perennial beacon of Christian virtue and leadership. His life, replete with divine inspiration and human sagacity, stands as an eternal testament to the transformative power of faith and the guiding light of divine providence.

Thus, we conclude this exploration of Pope Leo the Great, with hearts uplifted and minds enlightened, forever inspired by his indelible imprint on the tapestry of history and the enduring legacy of his saintly life.

Appendix A: Appendix

In this appended portion of our discourse, we endeavor to furnish both an archival timeline detailing the venerable life of Pope Leo I and a compendium of his pivotal documents and missives, which resonate through the corridors of ecclesiastical history. By charting the salient milestones from his nativity unto his ascension and ensuing deeds, we aim to encapsulate the transformative epochs of his earthly sojourn. The collected writings, a testament to divine eloquence and sagacity, reveal his indomitable spirit and theological acumen. Through this, one might perceive the magnitude of his influence, rendering a profound appreciation of his role in sculpting the bedrock of the Holy Church and the moral edifice of Christendom.

Timeline of Pope Leo I's Life

Pope Leo I, also known as Leo the Great, was born in the vicinity of Rome around the year 400 AD. From an early age, he exhibited signs of piety and intellectual prowess, traits that would guide him through his ecclesiastical journey. He came of age at a time when the Roman Empire was teetering on the brink of decline, yet his early experiences would instill in him a deeply rooted sense of duty towards preserving the sanctity of the Church.

By the time Leo reached his twenties, he had already embarked upon his religious vocation, demonstrating a profound commitment to the faith. Through service in various clerical capacities, he honed his theological and administrative skills, which would later become instrumental during his papacy. It was during these formative years that Leo cultivated relationships with key ecclesiastical figures, setting the stage for his future influence within the Church.

Leo's rise within the Church hierarchy was rapid and marked by steadfast dedication. In 431 AD, he was ordained a deacon and soon thereafter began serving as a senior advisor to Pope Celestine I. His role expanded significantly under Pope Sixtus III, who recognized Leo's potential and appointed him as an intermediary during church disputes. This position allowed Leo to develop a keen understanding of ecclesiastical diplomacy and solidify his reputation as a figure of authority and wisdom within the Church.

In the year 440 AD, the mantle of supreme pontiff fell upon Leo. His ascension to the papacy occurred at a turbulent time, both politically and religiously. The Roman Empire was in decay, and various heresies threatened the unity of Christendom. Leo's initial acts as pope involved bolstering the integrity of the Church's teachings and countering heretical movements, emphasizing the need for doctrinal purity and unity under papal authority.

Throughout his pontificate, Leo tirelessly advanced theological and ecclesiastical reforms. In 451 AD, he played a pivotal role at the Council of Chalcedon. His Tome, a document that articulated the dual nature of Christ, was central to the council's decrees, underscoring Leo's theological acumen and his capacity to influence the broader Christian doctrine. The council's endorsement of his teachings solidified his legacy as a defender of orthodoxy.

Pope Leo's political influence was perhaps most vividly illustrated in 452 AD, when he famously negotiated with Attila the Hun. By confronting the feared invader at the gates of Rome, Leo's diplomacy and moral authority not only spared the city from destruction but also reinforced his stature as a protector of the faith and the temporal realms. This encounter is often celebrated as a testament to his skillful interplay between spiritual leadership and worldly affairs.

Amidst these grand gestures, Leo also focused on internal reforms within the Church. He initiated structural changes to strengthen ecclesiastical organization and discipline. His efforts to regulate the clergy and laity aimed to fortify the moral foundation of the Church. By emphasizing the pastoral responsibilities of bishops and the sanctity of clerical conduct, Leo sought to instill a sense of piety and rectitude that resonated through the centuries.

Leo's pontificate was marked by prolific writings and sermons, through which he articulated his theological vision and pastoral concerns. His homilies often addressed the pressing issues of his time, offering guidance and solace to his flock. The elegance and rhetorical power of his words reflected his philosophical background and his commitment to conveying the truths of the faith with clarity and conviction.

Despite Pope Leo's accomplishments, his papacy was not devoid of challenges. The decline of the Roman Empire brought about political and social upheaval that demanded his constant vigilance. Internal conflicts within the Church, disputes with other ecclesiastical jurisdictions, and the ever-present threat of heretical doctrines required a leader of steadfast resolve and wisdom. Leo met these challenges with a fortitude that earned him enduring reverence and admiration.

Leo's final years were a testament to his enduring spirit and unwavering commitment to the Church. With the same vigor that characterized his earlier years, he continued to advocate for ecclesiastical unity and doctrinal purity. When he passed away on November 10, 461 AD, the Church mourned the loss of a truly great leader. However, his legacy was far from over, as his contributions continued to shape the trajectory of Christian doctrine and ecclesiastical governance.

In recognition of his saintly virtues and monumental impact, Leo was canonized and came to be known as Saint Leo the Great. His sanctification was a reflection of the profound reverence he garnered during his life and the centuries that followed. Through his tireless efforts and unparalleled leadership, Pope Leo I left an indelible mark on the history of the Church, a legacy that endured through time and memory.

As historians and Roman Catholics reflect upon the life of Pope Leo the Great, it becomes clear that his influence extended beyond the temporal realm. His theological contributions, political acumen, and pastoral care exemplify a life devoted to the service of God and the Church. The timeline of his life serves as a chronicle not only of a single man's journey but of a pivotal era in the annals of Christian history.

Key Documents and Writings by Pope Leo I

The legacy of Pope Leo I, known to history as Leo the Great, is preserved in an array of documents and writings, testament to his intellectual vigor and pastoral strength. These works, steeped in theological insight and practical wisdom, continue to resonate within the annals of Church history, offering deep reflections on faith, doctrine, and ecclesiastical governance. Among these writings, his letters, sermons, and doctrinal treatises stand out as pivotal texts that have shaped the development of orthodox Christian thought.

It is within the confines of his letters, or *epistolae*, that Leo's erudition and strategic acumen shine most vividly. These epistles, addressed to various clerics, laypeople, and political figures, are not mere correspondences but carefully crafted theological and canonical discourses. One notable example is his *Tome to Flavian*, a document of paramount importance in the Christological debates of the time. In this letter, Leo articulated the doctrine of the two natures of Christ—fully divine and fully human, unified in one person—thus, providing a cornerstone for the Council of Chalcedon in 451 A.D. and affirming the orthodox faith against the Eutychian heresy.

Beyond his letters, Pope Leo's sermons are imbued with a linguistic elegance and spiritual fervor rarely matched. Delivered with rhetorical mastery, these homilies often addressed liturgical seasons and feasts, aiming to instruct the faithful and fortify their piety. One finds in his sermons a profound meditation on the mysteries of the Incarnation, Passion, and Resurrection of Christ. His Christmas Sermons, in particular, are celebrated for their theological profundity and poetic expression, conveying the awe and reverence due to the birth of the Savior.

Among the copious sermon collections, over ninety have been preserved, revealing Leo's profound scriptural knowledge and pastoral sensitivity. Each sermon, whether expounding on the diligence required of a bishop or the virtue of charity among Christians, bears his distinctive theological insights and moral exhortations. Leo's eloquence, characterized by its clarity and precision, bridges the divine mysteries with the experiences of his flock, nurturing a deeper spiritual and intellectual connection to their faith.

The doctrinal treatises of Pope Leo, albeit fewer than his other writings, were equally influential. His works aimed to delineate the orthodoxy of Christian beliefs against the backdrop of rampant heresies and theological confusions of his time. One cannot overlook his treatise on the "Hypostatic Union," where he elaborated on the conjoined yet distinct nature of Christ's humanity and divinity—a concept still central to Christian doctrine today. These treatises were not mere theoretical constructs but practical guides for the Church's teaching authority, aiding bishops and priests in upholding doctrinal purity and unity.

In essence, Leo's writings are not confined to the theoretical or philosophical; they are imbued with practical guidance for the governance of the Church. His correspondence with the Gallican and African churches, aiming to resolve ecclesiastical disputes and enforce canonical discipline, showcases his commitment to maintaining ecclesial unity. His interventions often emphasized the primacy of the Roman See, asserting its role as the guardian of orthodoxy and arbiter of ecclesiastical matters.

The corpus of texts attributed to Pope Leo I also extends to his rule and methodologies for the administration of sacraments, providing instructional guidance for the clergy. His directives concerning the observance of Lent and the celebration of Easter are reflective of his intent to cultivate uniformity in liturgical practices. By standardizing these practices, Leo sought to foster a cohesive and spiritually enriched Christian community.

Another significant aspect of Leo's writings is his engagement with secular authorities, which illustrates his adeptness in navigating the complex interplay between the sacred and secular realms. His letters to Emperor Valentinian III and Empress Pulcheria reveal his role in influencing imperial policies and protecting the interests of the Church. These correspondences highlight Leo's political astuteness and his ability to wield theological arguments to achieve ecclesiastical and social objectives.

Moreover, Leo's attempts at ecclesiastical reform are intricately documented in his writings. His efforts to discipline clergy and laity alike are articulated through a series of letters and decrees that aimed to rectify moral lapses and enforce clerical celibacy. These documents, while addressing specific incidents, reflect a broader vision of a disciplined and morally upright ecclesiastical body, capable of embodying and propagating the Christian virtues.

Leo's writings are impregnated with a sense of urgency and mission, reflective of the turbulent times in which he lived. The decline of the Roman Empire, the threat of invasions, and internal ecclesiastical strife form the backdrop against which these documents were penned. Hence, his writings offer more than theological expositions; they are historical artifacts that provide insights into the socio-political and religious milieu of the fifth century.

One can locate in Pope Leo's works a vivid portrayal of his pastoral heart, a shepherd leading his flock amidst chaos and confusion. His words, framed in the classical elegance reminiscent of Cicero, imbued with the spiritual depth of Augustine, and bearing the authoritative tone of an ecclesiastical father, resonate with a timeless appeal. These documents are not mere relics of a bygone era but living texts, continuing to inform and inspire those who delve into their depths.

In conclusion, the documents and writings of Pope Leo I stand as a monumental testament to his intellectual and spiritual legacy. They encapsulate his theological acumen, pastoral wisdom, and ecclesiastical authority, offering rich resources for understanding the evolution of Christian doctrine and the historical dynamics of the early Church. For historians, theologians, and the faithful alike, these texts provide an invaluable window into the mind and heart of one of Christianity's greatest pontiffs.

Glossary of Terms

This glossary provides definitions and explanations of key terms and phrases relevant to the life, theological contributions, and historical significance of Pope Leo the Great. It serves to elucidate the lexicon and establish a foundational understanding of terminologies that are quintessential for comprehending this era and its ecclesiastical context.

Attila the Hun

The formidable ruler of the Huns who led invasions across Europe during the 5th century. He is famously known for his encounter with Pope Leo I, which purportedly led to the retreat of the Huns from Italy, staving off potential destruction.

Catechumen

An individual undergoing instruction and preparation for baptism into the Christian faith. During Pope Leo's time, catechumens were meticulously educated in the doctrines and practices of the Church.

Christology

The theological study concerning the nature and role of Christ. Pope Leo I made significant contributions to Christology, particularly with his Tome of Leo, which articulated the dual nature of Christ as both fully divine and fully human.

Ecumenical Council

A formal assembly of church officials and theologians aimed at resolving doctrinal and ecclesiastical issues. The Council of Chalcedon (451 AD), influenced greatly by Pope Leo's theological positions, is a prime example.

Heresy

A belief or opinion that deviates from the established doctrines of the church. Pope Leo I was a staunch defender of orthodox Christian beliefs and combated various heresies that threatened church unity.

Infallibility

The doctrine that, in specific circumstances, the Pope is free from error when pronouncing dogma concerning faith and morals. Pope Leo's authoritative theological positions were foundational in discussions about papal infallibility.

Pontificate

The period during which a particular pope reigns. Pope Leo's pontificate, from 440 to 461 AD, was marked by significant theological, political, and social contributions to the church and the broader Roman society.

The Tome of Leo

A letter written by Pope Leo I to the Council of Chalcedon, elucidating the nature of Christ as being both fully divine and fully human. This document was critical in shaping Christological doctrine and promoting church unity.

Trinitarian Doctrine

The Christian belief in the Trinity, that God exists as three persons in one essence: the Father, the Son, and the Holy Spirit. Pope Leo's teachings often reinforced this core tenet of Christian theology.

Vulgate

The Latin translation of the Bible, primarily completed by St. Jerome in the late 4th century. During Pope Leo's era, the Vulgate was instrumental in the education and liturgical practices of Western Christianity.

www.ingramcontent.com/pod-product-compliance
Lightning Source LLC
Chambersburg PA
CBHW080744120726
48001CB00009B/2681